checkpoint

Endorsed by
**University of Cambridge
International Examinations**

english
2

Sue Hackman   Alan Howe
Revised by Sue Bonnett

**HODDER
EDUCATION**
PART OF HACHETTE LIVRE UK

ACKNOWLEDGEMENTS

The Publishers would like to thank the following for permission to reproduce copyright material:

Photo credits:
Cover © Andrew Brookes/Corbis; **p.17** © Bob Battersby/BDI Images; **p.23** Mary Evans Picture Library; **p.41** Hodder Wayland 1995; **p.59** The Bridgeman Art Library; **p.81** Shakespeare Centre Library Stratford-Upon-Avon; **p.83** The Bridgeman Art Library; **p.86** © Corbis-Bettman; **p.97** *from top to bottom* © Corbis, © Greenpeace, © Holt Studios/Inga Spence; **p.102** © Holt Studios/Inga Spence.

Text credits:
p.6 'Thirteen questions you should be prepared to answer if you lose your ears at school' © John Coldwell; **p.14** 'The Commentator' from *Song of the City* © Gareth Owen, 1985, Collins; **p.20** 'Mary Celeste' © Judith Nicholls, Faber and Faber; **p.24** *tl* 'Fairy Story' from *Collected Poems* by Stevie Smith © Estate of James MacGibbon; *tr* 'The Listeners' from *Complete Poems* by Walter de la Mare © The Literacy Trustees of Walter de la Mare and the Society of Authors as their representative; *cl* 'The Malfeasance' © Alan Bold; *cr* 'Annabel Lee' by Edgar Allan Poe, *bl* 'Inchcape Rock' by Robert Southey, *bc* 'The Lady of Shalott' by Alfred Lord Tennyson, *br* 'Child Maurice'; **pp.26, 27, 28, 29** 'Beowulf and the Fire Dragon' from *Beowulf the Warrior* by Ian Serraillier © Anne Serraillier, originally published by Oxford University Press, 1954; **p.35** 'The Day I Wore High Heels' by Anna Cartwright from *Cambridge Young Writers: I'm Telling You* © Cambridge University Press and the Authors, 2000; **p.38** *Buddy* © Nigel Hinton, 1983, Orion Children's Books; **pp.47–55, 61, 63** 'The Ice Maiden' from *Thirteen Unpredictable Tales* © Paul Jennings, 1997, Penguin Australia; **p.58** 'First Love' by John Clare; **p.60** 'Valentine' is taken from *Mean Time* by Carol Ann Duffy, published by Anvil Press Poetry in 1993; **pp.107–108** cartoons from www.oneworld.com © Anne Ward; **p.114** *The Barking Ghost* © R L Stine, 1995, Scholastic Inc.

t = top, b = bottom, l = left, r = right, c = centre

Every effort has been made to trace all copyright holders, but if any have been inadvertently overlooked the Publishers will be pleased to make the necessary arrangements at the first opportunity.

Although every effort has been made to ensure that website addresses are correct at time of going to press, Hodder Murray cannot be held responsible for the content of any website mentioned in this book. It is sometimes possible to find a relocated web page by typing in the address of the home page for a website in the URL window of your browser.

Orders: please contact Bookpoint Ltd, 130 Milton Park, Abingdon, Oxon OX14 4SB. Telephone: (44) 01235 827720. Fax: (44) 01235 400454. Lines are open from 9.00 to 5.00, Monday to Saturday, with a 24-hour message answering service. Visit our website at www.hoddereducation.co.uk.

© Sue Hackman, Alan Howe, Sue Bonnett, 2005
First published in 2002 as *New Hodder English Gold 2*
This title first published in 2005 by
Hodder Education, part of Hachette Livre UK.
338 Euston Road
London NW1 3BH

Impression number	10 9 8 7 6 5
Year	2010 2009 2008

All rights reserved. Apart from any use permitted under UK copyright law, the material in this publication is copyright and cannot be photocopied or otherwise produced in its entirety or copied onto acetate without permission. Electronic copying is not permitted. Permission is given to teachers to make limited copies of pages 14–16, 57, 66, 70–74, 76–78, 91, 94, 97 and 101 for classroom distribution only, to students within their own school or educational institution. The material may not be copied in full, in unlimited quantities, kept on behalf of others, distributed outside the purchasing institution, copied onwards, sold to third parties, or stored for future use in a retrieval system. This permission is subject to the payment of the purchase price of the book. If you wish to use the material in any way other than as specified you must apply in writing to the Publisher at the above address.

Typeset in 13 on 20pt New Century Schoolbook by Fakenham Photosetting Limited, Fakenham, Norfolk
Illustrations by Kate Sardella of Ian Foulis & Associates (Units Two, Three and Five); p95 Anne Ward.
Cover design by John Townson/Creation
Printed in Malaysia

A catalogue record for this title is available from the British Library

ISBN: 978 0340 887 387

CONTENTS

Acknowledgements	ii
Introduction	iv
Checkpoint English Curriculum Objectives	vi
Teacher Guidance	viii
Unit One: Talking Teams	**1**
Unit Two: Narrative Poetry	**13**
Unit Three: Editor	**31**
Unit Four: The Ice Maiden	**43**
Unit Five: Smart Reading	**69**
Unit Six: Shakespeare's Theatre	**81**
Unit Seven: Marvel or Monster? Right or Wrong?	**95**
Unit Eight: Horror	**107**
Usage Activities	125
Usage Answers	145

INTRODUCTION

Welcome to *Checkpoint English*, which comprises three fully revised editions adapted from books in the *Hodder English Gold* series. *Checkpoint English 1* introduces pupils to a wide and challenging variety of English experiences and assignments, which are then progressively built on and broadened in *Checkpoint English 2* and *3*. However, teachers may wish to use these books to supplement their own schemes of work, or other materials.

Raising standards and covering curriculum requirements

We have taken as our prime directive the advancement of pupil learning. All the materials in *Checkpoint English* offer the very best of current practice. We know that pupils in the early levels of literacy need explicit instruction and scaffolded activities. We have provided both in the context of purposeful work and quality texts. Each book contains one unit of work that addresses basic skills as a focus of work in its own right and consolidation activities have been built in later. The units are therefore very suitable to address the Reading, Writing, Usage, and Speaking and Listening objectives of the CIE Checkpoint English Curriculum.

Checkpoint English addresses the appropriate number of set texts and includes many more. Pre-twentieth-century literature is amply represented in both fiction and non-fiction. You will find a catholic range of genres, tones and forms, but we have resisted simplified versions in favour of abridgement. Although speaking and listening is not tested at this level, the Checkpoint curriculum maintains that its importance in language development is such that it should play a major part in the curriculum alongside reading and writing. Therefore, we have made particular efforts to ensure that speaking and listening is fully represented in the series, not merely as incidental group talk but as a purposeful activity in its own right.

Structure

Checkpoint English consists of three books and a CD. Each book is divided into units, which have been arranged across the three years to establish, revisit and consolidate key skills.

Although the units have been placed in an order that offers pupils a varied and progressive experience of English, you can use the book in a flexible way, linking units with others or with texts you want to teach.

Whilst we have introduced basic skills directly through units, we also assume that teachers will continue to support individual pupils by giving them feedback on their oral and written performance, and that spelling, punctuation and grammar will be part of this continuing work. The Usage sections for each unit have activities with a more focused attention on sentence structure, grammar, punctuation and spelling, and vocabulary. Unit Four in *Checkpoint English 3* gives advice and activities for preparing for the Checkpoint English tests.

Progression

Checkpoint English 1, 2 and *3* form an incremental programme of work with clear goals written with the expressed intention of raising standards in English. The course offers far more than a sequence of self-contained lessons or starting points because progression is built into each unit, between each book and across the course as a whole. Key elements of English are focused on once in each year, and incidentally as a part of other units.

Assessment

Assessment is an integral part of each unit. However, checklists, recording sheets and assessment grids are deliberately not included, as it is most likely that you have already developed a workable system. Teaching by units enables you to collect evidence of pupils' achievements periodically, and systematically, at the end of each unit. The book provides the pupils with focused tasks and explicit criteria for evaluating how well they are doing, and what they need to improve on.

Activities

The initial material and activities of each unit are designed to introduce pupils to the focus for the sequence of work, and to engage their interest. There is then a series of tasks designed to help pupils to develop specific areas of knowledge, understanding and skill. Several pages are given to consolidating new knowledge or skills in context.

Using *Checkpoint English*

Many of the units are free-standing and teachers will find them sufficiently flexible to introduce extra material or to extend their use beyond a half-term. Texts have been chosen for their quality and for their richness in classroom study, as well as for their accessibility, and relevance for the age group. Where it has been impractical to reproduce whole texts, we have produced extracts to support the close study of key passages.

In addition, the CD provides support where it is most helpful. To promote reading skills, we recommend that pupils conduct close study activities using the text as well as the CD so that they can learn how to find particular words, phrases and information in the text. Where the CD icon appears (shown on the right) the text which is being studied is provided on the CD as well.

For your convenience, a number of pages have been designed as *photocopiable*. These pages contain activities that pupils will do best if they are involved in hands-on work.

CHECKPOINT ENGLISH CURRICULUM OBJECTIVES

Introduction

The teaching of English should develop pupils' abilities to use language effectively, to communicate in speech and in writing and to respond with understanding and insight to a wide range of texts. Whilst speaking and listening is not tested at this level, its importance in language development is such that it should play a major part in the curriculum alongside reading and writing. An integrated curriculum is envisaged in which speaking and listening activities commonly support learning.

Reading

Pupils should:

- Read a wide range of narrative, non-fiction and media texts. These may include novels, short stories, drama scripts, poetry, journals, diaries, letters, leaflets, magazines, newspapers and advertising matter
- Recognise explicit meaning, select, collate and summarise facts and ideas, using their own words where appropriate to demonstrate understanding
- Recognise and comment on opinions expressed by a writer
- Understand vocabulary and comment on a writer's use of language, such as the use of an informal or a formal style, or the choice of words to create an atmosphere or to persuade the reader
- Recognise implied meaning, such as the inference of character from what someone says or does in a text, or the meaning contained in an image
- Comment on the main features of narrative writing, such as character, setting, theme, and the way in which a plot is put together
- Demonstrate understanding of features of narrative, non-fiction and media texts by developing them in their own discussion and writing, for example, a further episode about a family portrayed in a book, or providing the wording for an advertisement

Writing

Pupils should:

- Write for a variety of purposes, such as to inform, explain, describe, explore, imagine, entertain, argue, persuade, instruct, analyse, review and comment
- Write in a wide range of forms, such as stories, poems, playscripts, autobiographies, personal letters, diaries, formal letters, persuasive writing, advertising copy, newspaper reports and articles, reviews, arguments, information sheets, notes and leaflets
- Begin to develop a sense of audience and to engage the reader's attention
- Structure their writing, using paragraphs and sequencing events, details and ideas within paragraphs
- Use varying styles of writing appropriate to different forms

Usage

Pupils should:

- Use full stops, capital letters, commas and question marks to make meaning clear, and show awareness of other forms of punctuation, including the presentation of dialogue
- Spell correctly most of the words they use
- Learn a range of vocabulary appropriate to their needs, and use vocabulary in speech and in writing to clarify meaning and to interest their audience
- Use a range of increasingly complex sentence structures to communicate meaning and to give fluency to their speech and writing
- Use correct grammar, including tense, case and word order

Speaking and listening

Pupils should:

- Speak for a variety of purposes, such as to explain, describe, narrate, explore, analyse, imagine, discuss, argue and persuade
- Participate in speaking and listening activities in order to discuss and prepare assignments
- Begin to make significant contributions to group discussions and help to plan and to give group presentations
- Hold conversations with others on familiar subjects
- Develop the ability to listen courteously to others and to be sensitive to turn-taking
- Practise speaking fluently at an appropriate pace
- Practise speaking clearly at an appropriate volume
- Use a range of vocabulary and sentence structure to make speech interesting and convincing

TEACHER GUIDANCE

UNIT ONE: TALKING TEAMS

READING	WRITING	SPEAKING & LISTENING
		Evaluate own speaking
		Develop recount
		Commentary
		Evaluate own listening
		Listen for a specific purpose
		Evaluate own contributions
		Building on others
		Varied roles in discussion
		Evaluate own drama skills

TEACHING SEQUENCE

Lesson 1:	Word of mouth activity
Lessons 2–3:	Listening and following up
Lessons 4–5:	Questions
Lesson 6:	Working in a team – radio simulation
Lessons 7–9:	Working in a team – *Crimewatch*

TEACHERS' NOTES

This unit is almost entirely about talk. The chief role of the teacher is to get the groups off to an efficient, well-briefed start and to draw out the learning in the debriefing afterwards. Managing group discussion depends on:

- Efficient, well-planned starts – who sits with whom, how many in each group, etc. Come prepared.
- Clear time limits and time warnings to fit your lesson length.
- A strong emphasis on debriefing and reflection. Under no circumstances sacrifice the time for reflection – that is where the learning lies.

Note the contribution this unit makes to the school's citizenship curriculum.

Lesson 1: Watch out for the growing groups and where they will sit.

Lessons 2–5: It has been left to you how to manage the debriefings and sharing. These could be expanded to include shared writing, listening to and commenting on the poems.

Lesson 6: Groups of five need to gather round a table to ensure participation. Try to arrange it so that those who have not yet had prominent roles take on the job of editor or spokesperson.

Lessons 7–9: You will need a large space such as a studio or hall to act out the scene with the whole class. Choose reliable pupil actors, as the purpose of the first run-through is to help pupils visualise and fix the events. The class then splits into groups of around ten. If larger groups would be more convenient, you can add further parts, e.g. people waiting in a bus queue, shoppers passing by, more customers. Again, try to ensure that pupils take on a range of different roles. Writing facilities are needed for the middle session, so a move back to a classroom is advisable. The writing could easily take up an extra lesson, and it would expand easily to include a video camera to make the programme. You would have to match the number of groups to the cameras available.

UNIT TWO: NARRATIVE POETRY

READING	WRITING	SPEAKING & LISTENING
Implied and explicit meanings	Figurative language	Commentary
Development of key ideas	Rework in different forms	Dramatic techniques
Compare treatments of same theme		Collaborative presentation
Independent reading		
Literary conventions		

TEACHING SEQUENCE

Lessons 1–2:	Narrative structure (*The Commentator*)
Lessons 3–5:	Narrative and figurative language (*Mary Celeste*)
Lessons 6–9:	A range of narrative poems
Lesson 10–11:	Performance (*Beowulf*)

TEACHERS' NOTES

Lessons 1–2: For the writing, you could organise pupils into groups for communal writing, and join one or more groups for more focused work. Another alternative would be to write the first suggested poem as a whole class in shared writing, then ask pupils to work individually or in groups on the second poem. You will need to allow an extra lesson this way.

Lessons 6–9: Allow time to debrief on the generic features of narrative poems. An interesting extension is to research narrative lyrics in chart music. You will need to provide a range of narrative poems listed in the 'Independent reading' section. You could add more, especially if they introduce poets that pupils are likely to encounter later in their studies.

UNIT THREE: EDITOR

READING	WRITING	SPEAKING & LISTENING
Implied and explicit meanings	Effective planning	
Transposition	Anticipate reader reaction	
Influence of technology	Establish the tone	
	Experiment with conventions	

TEACHING SEQUENCE

Lessons 1–2:	Introduction and Task 1 (Telling tales)
Lessons 3–4:	Task 2 (Sexism)
Lessons 5–7:	Task 3 (From prose to picture)
Lessons 8–9:	Task 4 (Books on the box)
Lesson 10:	Task 5 (Cutting down)
Lesson 11:	Task 6 (Selling it like it is)

TEACHERS' NOTES

Task 1: Avoid the drudgery of rewriting, unless you can do it on word processors. Instead, ask pupils to do the tasks orally. The points are obvious and will emerge clearly enough. Focus your efforts on the debriefings.

To extend this unit, apply the tasks to recent class texts or texts that pupils bring in.

UNIT FOUR: THE ICE MAIDEN

READING	WRITING	SPEAKING & LISTENING
Note-making formats	Advice about options	Hypothesis and speculation
Versatile reading	Integrate evidence	Dramatic technique
Trace developments	Critical review	Work in role
Development of key ideas		
Compare treatments of same theme		
Interpret a text		

TEACHING SEQUENCE

Lesson 1:	Meet Paul Jennings and writer's style
Lesson 2:	Sections 1 and 2
Lesson 3:	Section 3
Lesson 4:	Section 4
Lesson 5:	What will happen next?
Lessons 6–7:	A look at love
Lesson 8:	Sections 5 and 6 and inventive endings
Lesson 9:	Using drama
Lesson 10:	Writing a review

TEACHERS' NOTES

A unit based around a Paul Jennings short story. The unit divides up the story into sections, interspersed with active reading and response activities that should provide for a lively series of shared reading sessions. The activities are specifically designed to promote open-ended discussion, and to sharpen pupils' abilities in learning to read beyond the lines. The ending of the story is deliberately separated out so that pupils can predict and reflect on their reading up to this point. Interspersed is a short section that takes a sideways look at the theme of love using a pre-twentieth-century poem followed by a twentieth-century poem for comparison. You should take the opportunity to gather a collection of other Paul Jennings books and encourage pupils to read more widely in order to gain a sense of the writer's distinctive style. You may wish to extend the unit with lessons devoted to group reading and discussion of other short stories.

UNIT FIVE: SMART READING

READING	WRITING	SPEAKING & LISTENING
Combine information	Writing to reflect	Evaluate own speaking
Independent research	Handwriting at speed	Format presentation
Note-making formats	Effective information	Hypothesis and speculation
Bias and objectivity		
Implied and explicit meanings		

TEACHING SEQUENCE

Lessons 1–3:	Introduction, choosing the candidates (reading skills)
Lesson 4:	Preparation of speaking cards
Lessons 5–8:	Preparing a presentation
Lessons 9–10:	Presentations and self-review

TEACHERS' NOTES

This unit teaches and requires pupils to employ a range of reading skills and strategies under the guise of a school-based version of the television series *Big Brother*, leading to a carefully planned oral presentation. The key text is a set of ten mini-biographies of prospective candidates, and time should be spent in the first series of lessons ensuring pupils have skimmed these, scanned for specific information, and read closely. The selection of candidates is an ideal activity to build around focused group discussion. Set pupils into project teams in order to carry out this task. You may need to provide support for the note-making skills required. To enhance the unit, you may wish to copy some of the resources such as 'speaking cards'. Provide plenty of time and coaching support for pupils as they work on and prepare their presentations. The final set of oral presentations will be enhanced if you can dramatise the situation by setting the classroom out as a meeting with the headteacher and school governors, with, if possible, an overhead projector or a laptop for PowerPoint and a screen.

UNIT SIX: SHAKESPEARE'S THEATRE

READING	WRITING	SPEAKING & LISTENING
Combine information	Effective information	Collaborative presentation
Independent research		
Note-making formats		
Historical context		
Cultural context		

TEACHING SEQUENCE

Lesson 1:	Shakespeare's life
Lessons 2–3:	Shakespeare's times
Lessons 4–5:	Shakespeare's theatre
Lessons 6–8:	Shakespeare's language

TEACHERS' NOTES

This is a short introductory unit to Shakespeare, designed to help pupils to gain a sense of the context in which the plays were written, and then tackle the language of the plays in an active way. Try to book the drama studio for the final series of lessons when language and scenes are being explored, although all activities can be undertaken in a classroom. Enhance the unit with different versions of the scenes from *Macbeth* on video, shown after pupils have worked on them themselves. Extend the unit by selecting further scenes to work on. Suitable candidates would include: Act 1 scene 5 of *Hamlet*; the end of Act 2 scene 2 in *Anthony and Cleopatra* (Enobarbus' description of Cleopatra in her barge); the workmen's performance of *Pyramus and Thisbe* in Act 5 scene 1 of *A Midsummer Night's Dream*.

UNIT SEVEN: MARVEL OR MONSTER? RIGHT OR WRONG?

READING	WRITING	SPEAKING & LISTENING
Combine information	Explain complex ideas	Formal presentation
Note-making formats	Present a case persuasively	Questions to clarify or refine
Trace developments	Develop an argument	Hidden messages
Bias and objectivity	Balanced analysis	Hypothesis and speculation
		Work in role

TEACHING SEQUENCE

Lesson 1:	Introduction to the issue: key concepts and vocabulary
Lesson 2:	Frankenfears – reading and response to pre-20th-century fictional account
Lesson 3:	Facts stranger than fiction – note-making
Lessons 4–5:	A moral maze – discussion and argument
Lesson 6:	Changing humans – close reading and note-making
Lessons 7–8:	Report writing
Lesson 9:	GM Crops – group discussion and analysis of two persuasive texts
Lessons 10–12:	The great crop debate

TEACHERS' NOTES

The focus of this unit is exploring an issue requiring the use of research and study skills in order to develop both written and oral explanation and argument. The central issue is the debate surrounding genetic engineering. You may need to explore the key concepts and vocabulary at the start of the unit.

Each of the texts will need to be taught in shared reading sessions, in order to support pupils with the combination of challenging language and ideas before they start work on independent tasks. Lessons 7–8 on report writing will need to be started with shared writing so that pupils can see the way a written report is planned and organised, and can be supported in using appropriate sentence structures. The debate at the end of the unit will need careful planning in order to create a sense of an authentic debate.

The extract from *Frankenstein*, which is used to create a context for the non-fictional material in this unit, is a useful foretaste of what is to come in the next unit.

UNIT EIGHT: HORROR

READING	WRITING	SPEAKING & LISTENING
Versatile reading	Narrative commentary	
Implied and explicit meanings	Figurative language	
Transposition	Establish the tone	
Influence of technology		
Compare treatments of same theme		
Literary conventions		

TEACHING SEQUENCE

Lessons 1–2:	Starts and settings (Beginnings, A place of horror and Horror train)
Lesson 3:	Monsters (Create your own monster)
Lessons 4–7:	Building suspense (Hanging on, Dead Man's Bay and Building up tension)
Lessons 8–11:	Horror writing (Dracula lives!, Horrible horror and The beast must die)
Lessons 12–13:	Graphic horror (From picture to page and From page to picture)

TEACHERS' NOTES

Pupils have a huge repertoire of knowledge about horror from a range of media. Use every opportunity to draw on this. Note also the resonance between this unit and the previous unit, 'Marvel or Monster?...'. The writing in Lessons 8–11 might be best done on a word processor, so that feedback can be sought and improvements accommodated.

UNIT ONE

Talking Teams

Word of mouth

Have you ever had a spooky experience?
For example:

- Something you dreamt about that came true
- Something you saw that couldn't be true
- A voice you heard when no one was there

Get into pairs and tell each other your strangest experience. Decide which one was best.

Now get into fours and tell the group the chosen story from each pair. The person telling the story should be the person who listened to it. Decide which one was best.

Get into eights and tell the group the chosen story from each foursome. The person telling the story should be someone who hasn't told it before. Decide which one was best.

As a class, listen to the 'winning' stories. The person telling the story should be someone who hasn't told it before. Decide which one was best.

Unit one

Time to reflect

Now get back into the group of four to discuss:

- What ingredients make a really fascinating story?
- What made the winning story the best story?
- What makes a good teller?
- What changes did you notice as the story was passed from teller to teller? Can you account for them?
- If you told a story, what did the listeners do to help?

> **HELP**
>
> Storytellers improve their stories each time they tell them by:
> - Building up suspense
> - Dwelling on fascinating details
> - Keeping the reader on tenterhooks
> - Adding in telling details
> - Finishing on a strong note

Listening checklist

How did you do as a listener? Try this test:

	Yes	Mostly	Sometimes	No
1. Did you make eye contact with the person telling the story?				
2. Did you nod and give encouragement?				
3. Did you face the storyteller and lean forward?				
4. Did your attention wander?				
5. If your attention did wander, did it show?				
6. Did you do anything that distracted the teller?				
7. Did you remember the openings?				
8. Did you remember the details in the middle?				
9. Did you remember the endings?				
10. Were you able to remember the sequence of events when you re-told a story?				

Set yourself two listening targets.

HELP

Tips for better listening:

- Look at the speaker
- Encourage the speaker, e.g. nod
- Show you are listening
- Talk back in your head
- Hunt for and remember the three or four main points
- Take notes if this is allowed – it keeps you focused and interested
- Work out when you tend to flag, and challenge yourself to stay on the ball.

Unit one

Follow-up questions

Get into groups of four and take turns to tell each other about a time when you thought you were in real danger. You only have a minute or two each.

On your own, write down a question for each person which will make them tell you something else about the event – something interesting.

Ask your questions, taking each person at a time.

Discussion

- Which of the follow-up questions were the most interesting?
- Which follow-up questions got the most interesting answers?
- Which follow-up questions got the longest answers?
- What makes a good follow-up question?

HELP

Good questions:

- Go to the heart of the matter
- Interest other people (make them think, 'I wish I'd asked that!')
- Don't have easy answers
- Reveal something new or important
- Help the speaker to make an important point

On the spot

Suggest some good follow-up questions for the cases below.

You are interviewing a famous politician about an epidemic that kills chickens. He says:

> This government recognises the threat to livestock and we are resolved to act quickly. We have called a meeting of key people to review the situation. We have alerted police and officials in the counties affected. We are contacting neighbouring counties so we can work in co-operation. I visited a chicken farm personally only this morning. We are doing everything we can to resolve the crisis.

You are a primary school teacher. Yema is nine years old and usually very happy and talkative. This week she is quiet and looks unhappy.

Teacher: Yema, you've not been your usual self this week. Is anything wrong?
Yema: Not really. Well, yes. It's… I can't…

Unit one

Unit one

Thirteen questions you should be prepared to answer if you lose your ears at school

Are they clearly named?
When did you notice they were missing?
Were they fixed on properly?
What colour are they?
What size?
Have you looked in the playground?
Did you take them off for P.E.?
Could somebody else have picked them up by mistake?
Have you felt behind the radiators?
Did you lend them to anybody?
Have you searched the bottom of your bag?
Does the person you sit next to have a similar pair?
Are you sure you brought them with you this morning?

John Coldwell

Activity

This poem is made up of questions.

- Think of three things that all the questions have in common.
- Think of three things the questions tell you about the person asking the questions.
- Think of three things the questions tell you about the person he or she is speaking to.

In a group, compose a similar poem made up of:

Questions a parent might ask if you want to go out with your friends for the evening

or

Questions a teacher might ask if you'd lost your homework (or so you say)

or

An idea of your own

Unit one

News team

Get into groups of five.

You are the news team at Eagle Radio.

There are ten news items for the next bulletin, but there is only time for six of them. The task for the team is to choose the six best stories.

1. Choose an **editor** who will listen to everyone's view then take a decision.
2. Choose a **spokesperson** who can explain your choices to the other groups.
3. Choose an **observer** who doesn't join in but does watch and take notes about the way the team works, and reports back later.
4. The rest of the team are **reporters** who will go out and report the news.

7

Unit one

The news stories

- A thirteen-year-old girl has just won a scholarship to the Royal School of Ballet.
- Viking swords discovered in local river by two girls.
- Workmen and motorists joined police to help clear 10,000 tin cans which fell from a lorry this morning.
- Local team has named their twelve players for the home game against Newtown on Saturday.
- Worries over safety of local canal.
- Fire destroys stables. Animals killed.
- Local boy claims UFO sighting.
- Pop star to open new skateboard park next week.
- Pupils at local high school collect over £5,000 for new hospital.
- Local hamster breaks world record for running in hamster wheel.

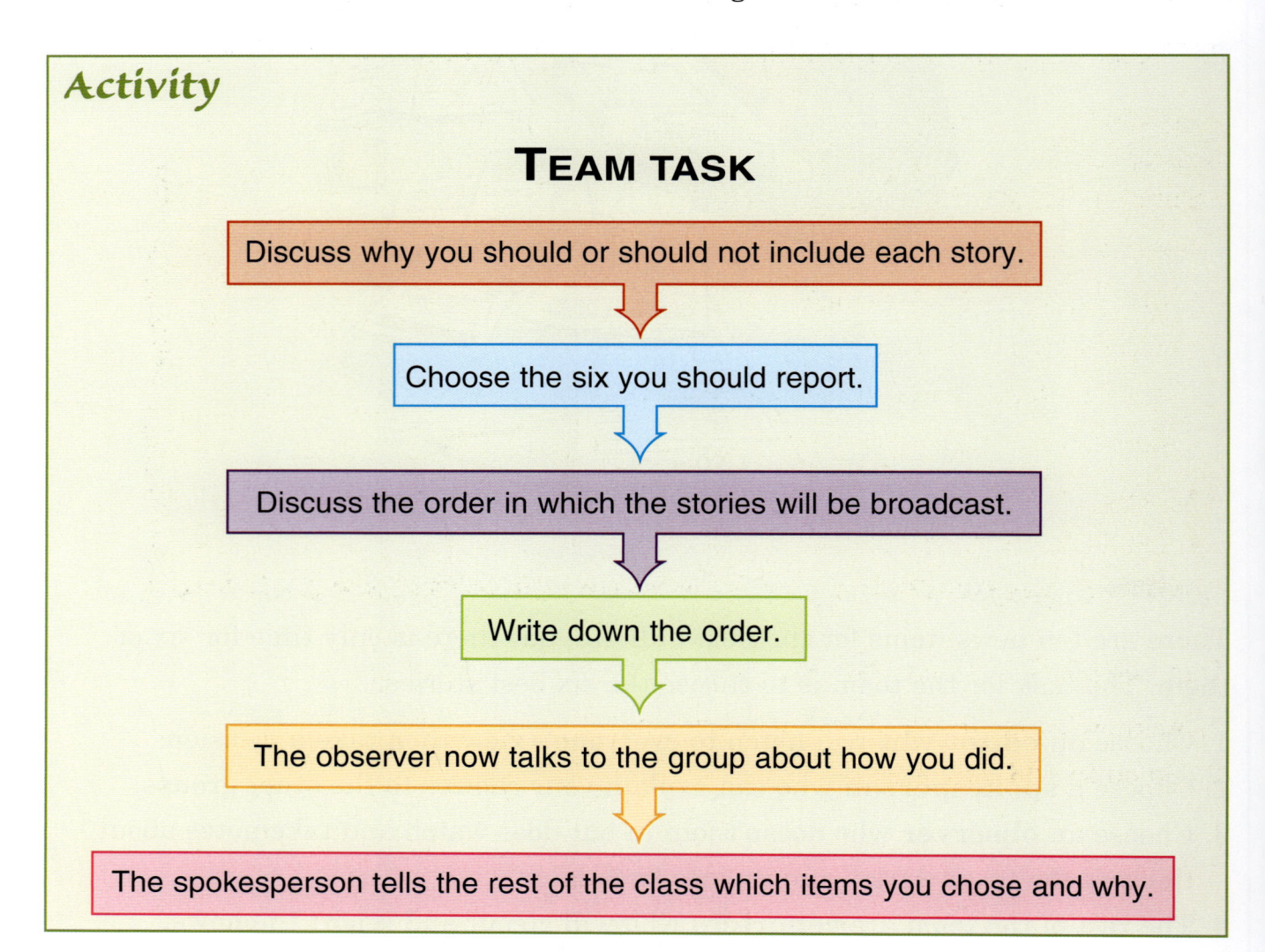

Activity

TEAM TASK

Discuss why you should or should not include each story.

↓

Choose the six you should report.

↓

Discuss the order in which the stories will be broadcast.

↓

Write down the order.

↓

The observer now talks to the group about how you did.

↓

The spokesperson tells the rest of the class which items you chose and why.

1. After doing this, make a list of the kind of things people do in discussions. For example:

    - Ask questions
    - Add to something someone else said
    - Agree with something someone else said
    - Suggest a new idea.

2. Make a note of the contributions you can remember making in the discussion. For example:

    I asked John what he meant.
    I argued to keep in the UFO story.
    I backed up Raisa's idea.

    What patterns can you see?

3. Choose one kind of contribution you never make and use it next time.

HELP

Building on others

Here are some phrases that will help you to follow up what others say:

- I think that's right because . . .
- Sally's right. The main point is . . .
- That's a good idea. An example would be . . .
- I think there's a problem with that because . . .
- I know what you mean, but . . .
- On the other hand . . .

Can you think of other phrases that:

1. Acknowledge what the last speaker said
2. Go on to add new ideas?

Unit one

Crimewatch

You are now going to act out a crime in the style of a reconstruction as seen on television.

Watch an example on television so you know the style of report.

Take the following roles:

- The presenter on *Crimewatch* who tells the story
- Two bank robbers
- A bank manager
- One person working at the till
- A driver sitting in a car outside the bank
- Two customers in the bank, one of whom is the driver's partner
- A couple of people chatting just outside the bank

This is the story:

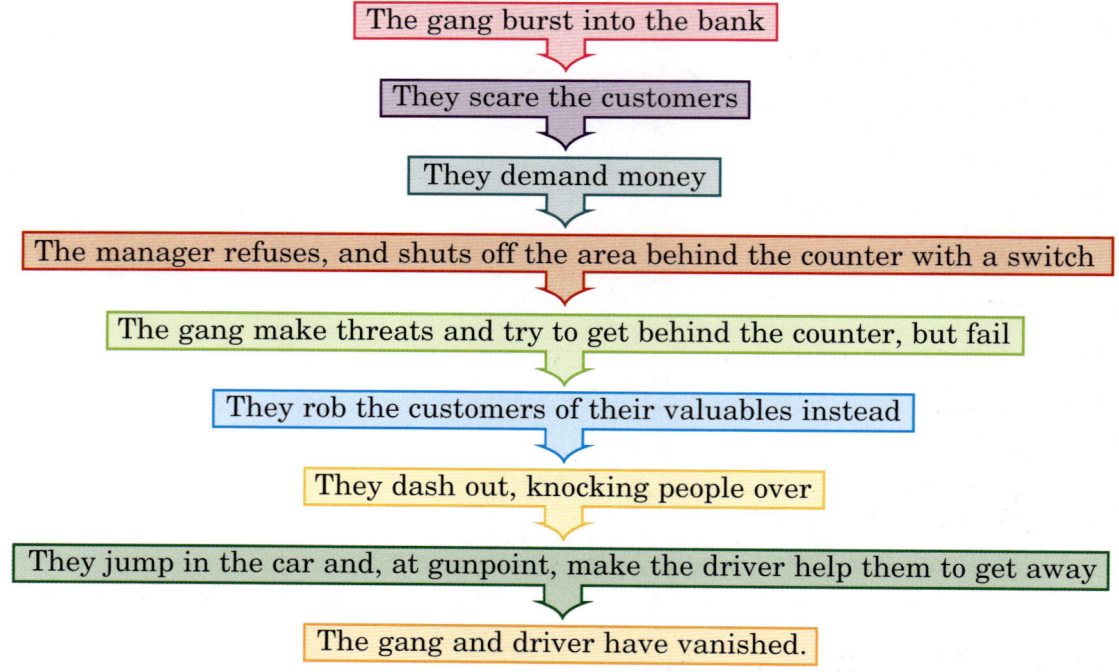

The gang burst into the bank

They scare the customers

They demand money

The manager refuses, and shuts off the area behind the counter with a switch

The gang make threats and try to get behind the counter, but fail

They rob the customers of their valuables instead

They dash out, knocking people over

They jump in the car and, at gunpoint, make the driver help them to get away

The gang and driver have vanished.

Unit one

Activity

1. Clear a big space and create a 'set'.
2. As a class, act out the event. Once may be enough. Your teacher will help you to get it right.
3. Get into groups of ten and decide how you would tell this story to the audience. Think about:
   - How the presenter will introduce the story
   - Which people to interview
   - How to build the story from interviews, reconstructed events and the presenter telling the story.
4. List the order of the scenes on a big sheet so everyone can see it.
   1. Presenter – set the scene
   2. Interview driver – dropping off partner, seeing men rush in
   3. Customer – seeing robbers enter bank – description
5. Perform the script with voices only – no need to act it – and see how it goes. Discuss changes to improve it.
6. Repeat this to get it right, and add in some scenes which you act. Your teacher will tell you if you can use a video camera for this.

Discuss:

- The skills that are needed to make this programme
- How you decide whether to show, tell or interview a person from each scene

How did you do?

	Yes	Mostly	Partly	No
1. Did you contribute your fair share to planning the programme?				
2. Did you take different types of role during this unit?				
3. Did you take a leading role at any time?				
4. Did you speak clearly?				
5. Did you get embarrassed or shy?				
6. Did it show?				
7. Did you improve your role each time you tried it?				
8. Did you change your voice successfully when you went into role?				
9. Did you change your behaviour successfully when you went into role?				
10. Were you able to speak formally when you had to?				

Set yourself two presentation targets.

UNIT TWO

Narrative Poetry

In the old days before people could read or write, stories were told by word of mouth.

The storyteller would:

- **Tell long tales of heroes and monsters, of battles and victories**
- **Make up story poems about big events**
- **Tell the tales as poems because the rhythm and the rhyme made them easier to remember.**

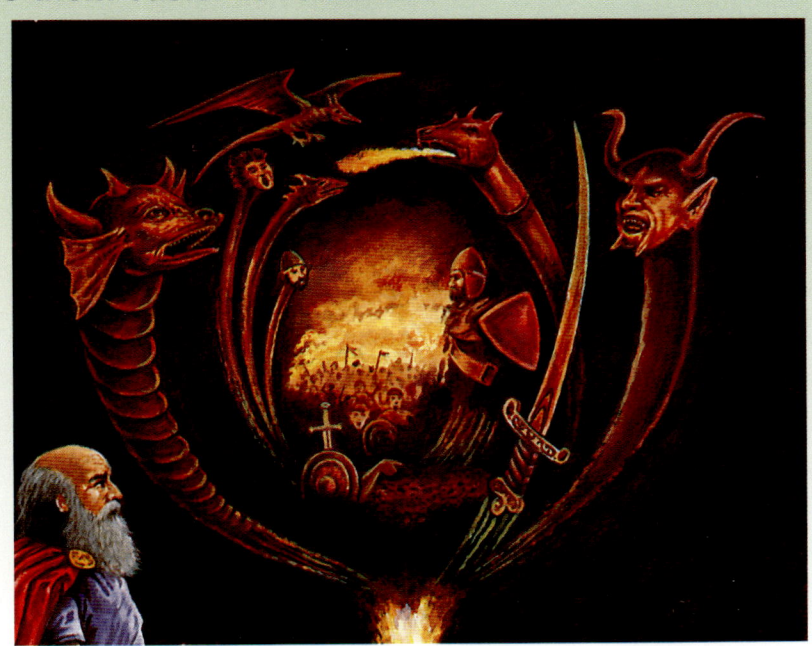

Unit two

The structure of a poem

Poems are often split up into sections. You can sometimes see this in the verses but you can also hear it when the tone or topic changes.

Look at the structure of this poem, in which a nine-year-old boy is pretending to be a football star.

The Commentator

Good afternoon and welcome,
This is Danny Markey your commentator
Welcoming you to this international
Between England and Holland,
Which is being played here this afternoon

At four Florence Terrace.
And the pitch looks in superb condition
As Danny Markey prepares
To kick off for England;
And this capacity crowd roars
As Markey, the England captain,
Puts England on the attack.

Straight away it's Markey
With a lovely pass to Keegan,
Keegan back to Markey,
Markey in possession now
Jinking skilfully past the dustbin
And a neat flick inside the cat there,
What a brilliant player this Markey is
And still only nine years old!

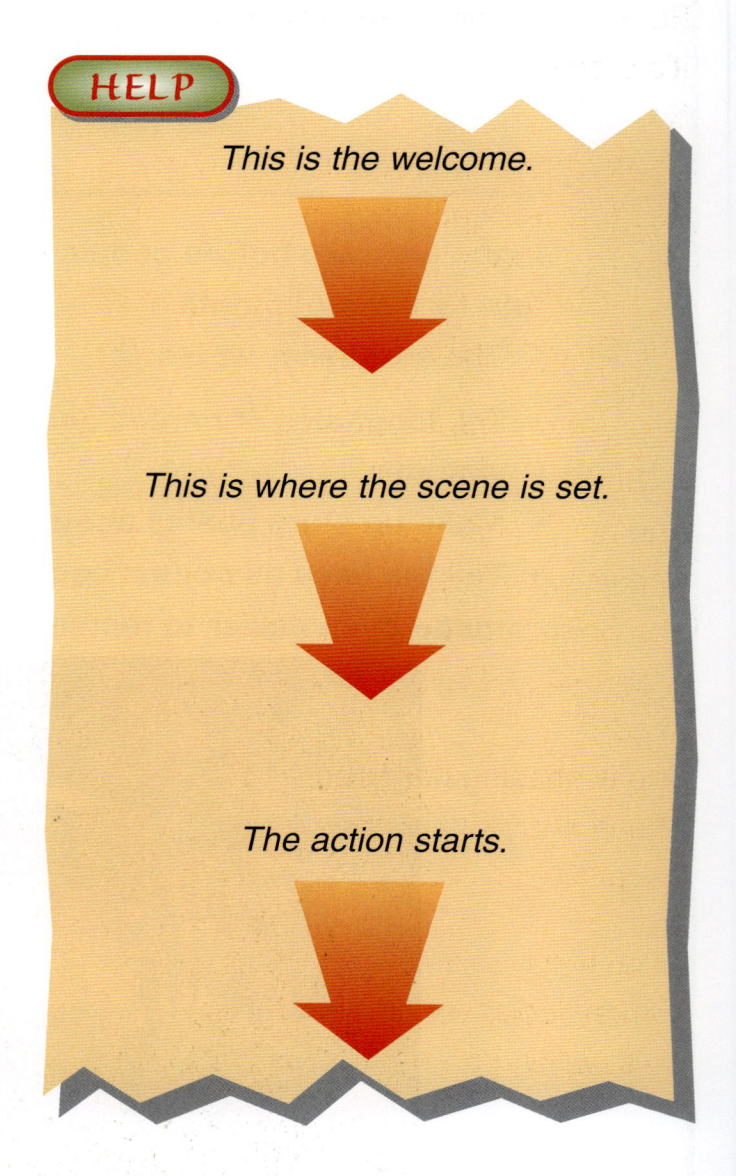

HELP

This is the welcome.

This is where the scene is set.

The action starts.

Unit two

Markey to Francis,
Francis to Markey,
Markey is through…
No, he's been tackled by the drainpipe;
But he's won the ball back brilliantly
And he's advancing on the Dutch keeper now,
It must be a goal,
He comes off his line
But Markey chips him brilliantly
It's a goal…
No.
It's gone into Mrs Spence's next door.
And Markey's going round
To ask for his ball back.

The Crowd is silent now.

If he can't get the ball back
It could be the end of this international.
And now the door's opening
And yes, it's Mrs Spence,
Mrs Spence has come to the door,
And wait a minute, she's shaking her head,
She is shaking her head,
She is not going to let Markey
Have his ball back.

What is the referee going to do?
Markey looks very dejected here,
He's walking back, hanging his head…

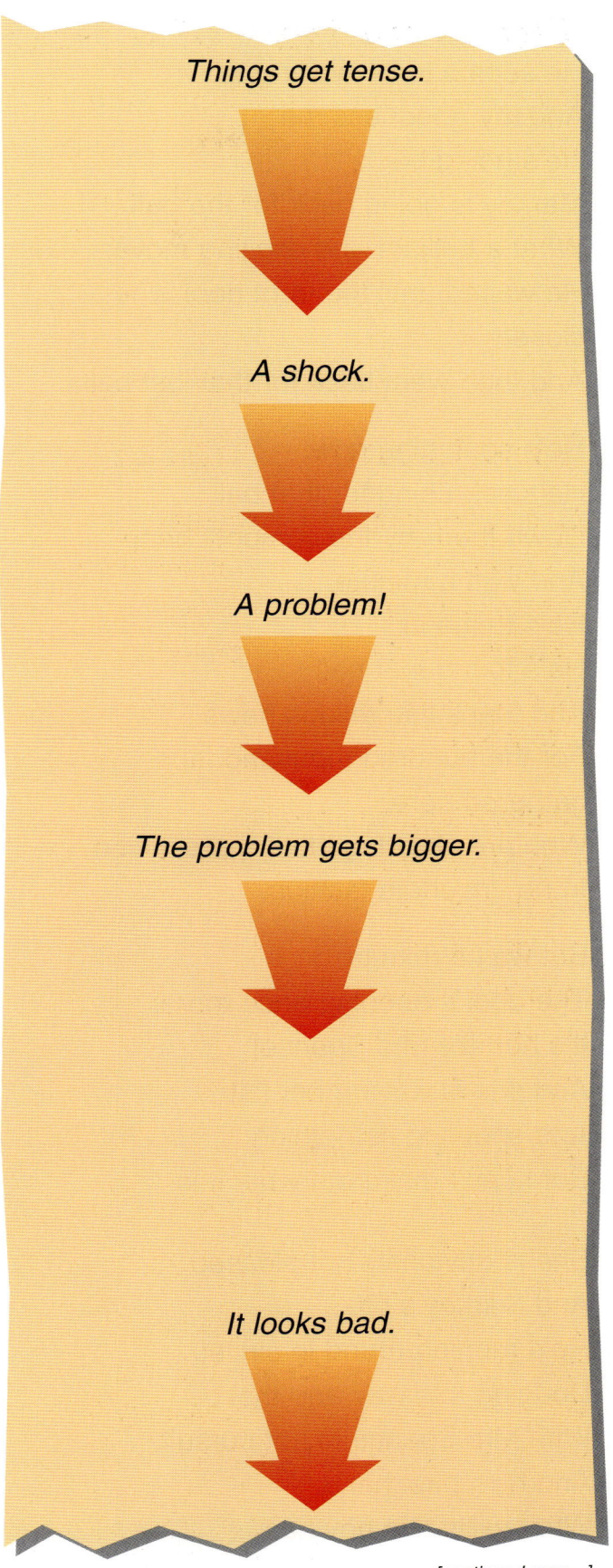

Things get tense.

⬇

A shock.

⬇

A problem!

⬇

The problem gets bigger.

⬇

It looks bad.

⬇

[continued over…]

Unit two

What's he doing now?
He seems to be waiting
And my goodness me
He's going back,
Markey is going back for the ball,
What a brilliant and exciting move;
He waited until the front door was closed
And then went back for that lost ball.

He's searching now,
He's searching for that ball
Down there by the compost heap
And wait a minute,
He's found it!
He's found that ball
And that's marvellous news
For the hundred thousand fans gathered here,
Who are showing their appreciation
In no uncertain fashion.

But wait a minute,
The door's opening once more;
It's her, it's Mrs Spence!
And she is waving her fist
And shouting something
But I can't make out what it is.

She is obviously not pleased.
And Markey's off,
He's running round in circles
Dodging this way and that
With Mrs Spence in hot pursuit,
And he's past her,
What skills this boy has.

Gareth Owen

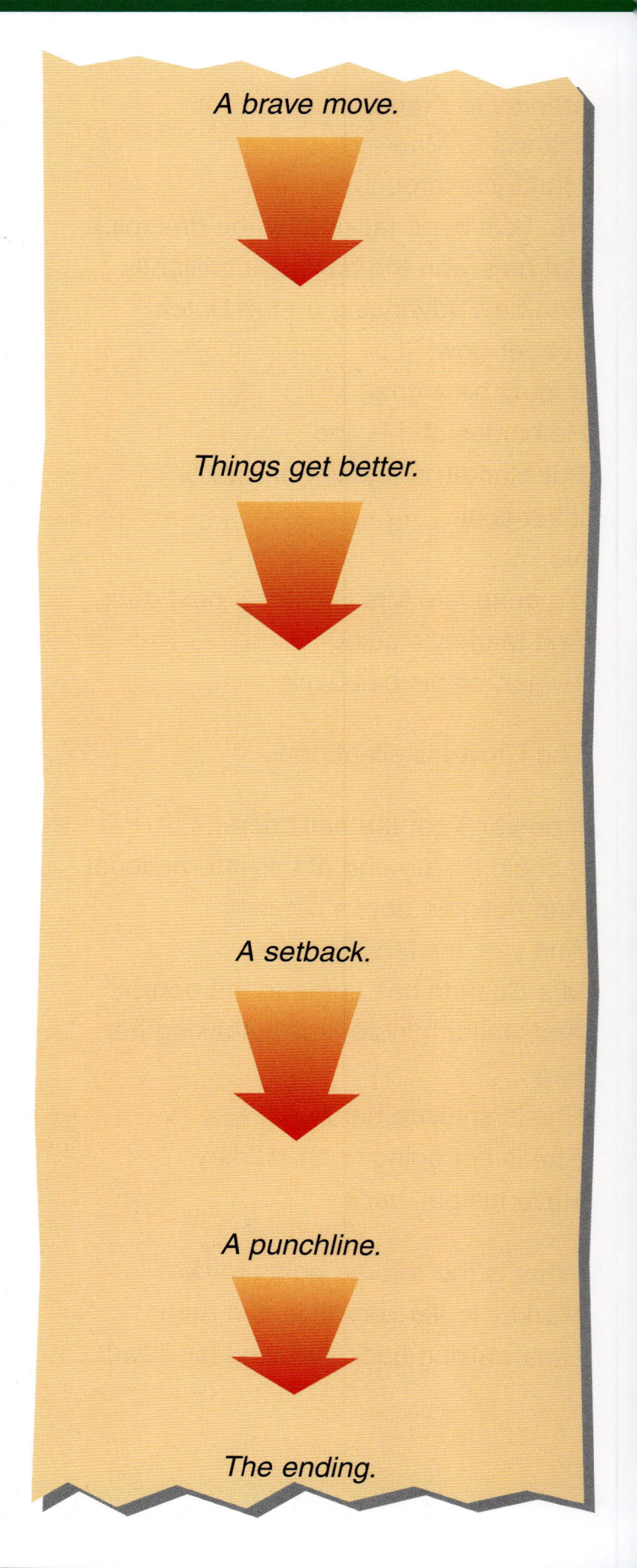

A brave move.

⬇

Things get better.

⬇

A setback.

⬇

A punchline.

⬇

The ending.

Checkpoint English 2 © HODDER MURRAY

Activity

- Read each section carefully. On a copy of the poem, use a coloured pencil to shade over every word that tells you that it is not a real match.
  For example:

  'At four Florence Terrace' because this sounds like someone's address and not the name of a famous football ground.

  'Dustbin' because you would not skilfully pass a ball around a dustbin.

- In a different colour, shade in the words that tell you that it sounds like a real match.
  For example:

  'As Markey, the England captain, puts England on the attack.'

- How should the poem sound? Have you heard sports' commentators? Discuss how they speak.

- Read the poem aloud as you think it should sound.

Unit two

Write your own!

Choose an event to write about.

If you are stuck, you may like to choose one of the following:

> **1 Sports' Commentator**
> Start like this:
> Good afternoon and welcome.
> This is _____ your commentator welcoming you to this _____ between _____ and _____...

or

> **2 Brit Awards Presenter**
> Start like this:
> Ladies and Gentlemen,
> welcome to the _____ Brit Awards, an evening of fabulous entertainment to celebrate British music.
> Tonight we are privileged to have with us all your favourite bands...

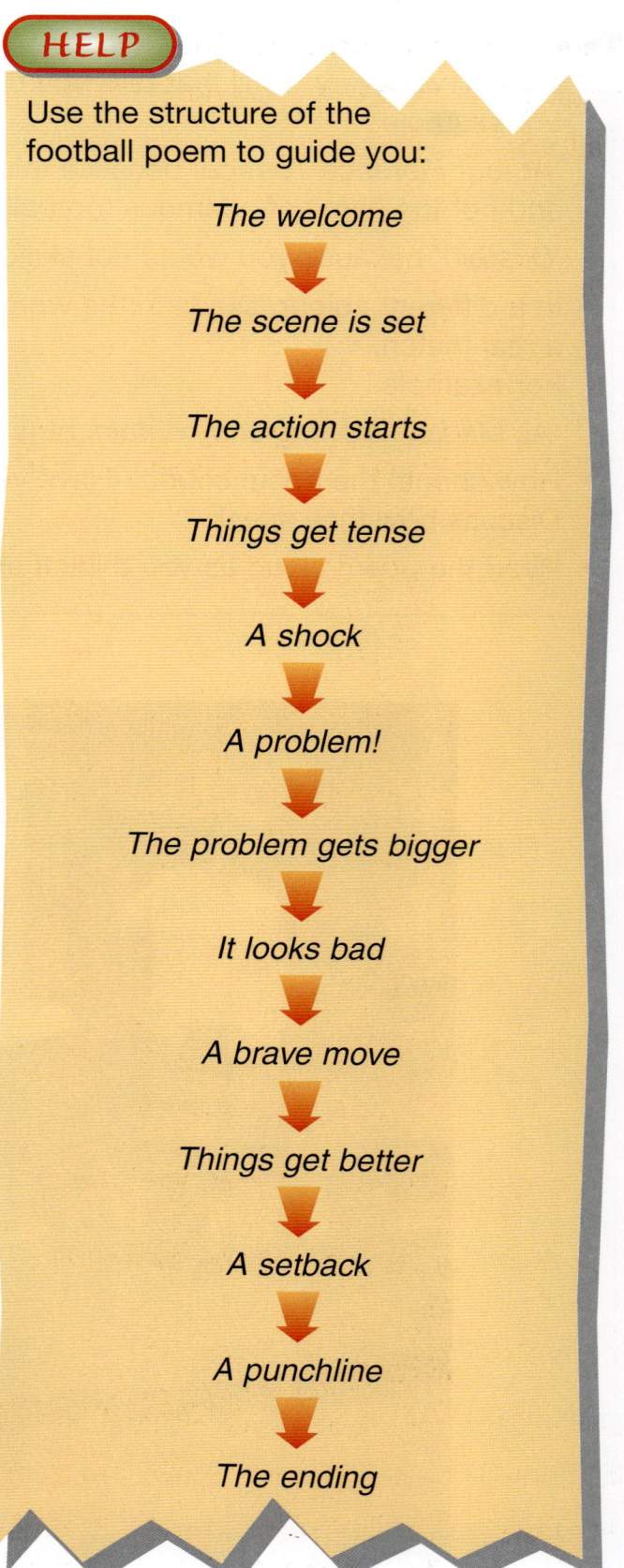

HELP

Use the structure of the football poem to guide you:

The welcome
⬇
The scene is set
⬇
The action starts
⬇
Things get tense
⬇
A shock
⬇
A problem!
⬇
The problem gets bigger
⬇
It looks bad
⬇
A brave move
⬇
Things get better
⬇
A setback
⬇
A punchline
⬇
The ending

The story of the *Mary Celeste*

This story of a ship called the *Mary Celeste* is a true story and a great mystery. Even today no one really knows what happened. Known facts about the *Mary Celeste*:

1. On 5 December the ship was found drifting on the ocean with no one on board.
2. The ship was in good condition and there was no sign of a struggle.
3. Some papers and the ship's boat were missing. However, clothes and other personal objects had been left including a rushed note from the mate to his wife.
4. There had been ten people on board including Captain Briggs, his wife and his baby daughter.
5. The ship had left New York on 7 November 1872.
6. The ship was sailing to Genoa, Italy, with a cargo of alcohol.
7. The last entry was written in the log book on 25 November.
8. It is known that there was a storm on the afternoon of 25 November.

Activity

- What do you think happened to the *Mary Celeste*?
- What happened to the people?
- How many explanations can you think of? Which do you think is the most likely?

Judith Nicholls wrote a poem about the story of the *Mary Celeste*. She used some of the facts that you have read. She also invented some details to make the poem more interesting.

You will find Judith Nicholls' poem on the next page.

Mary Celeste

*Only the wind sings
in the riggings,
the hull creaks a lullaby;
a sail lifts gently
like a message
pinned to a vacant sky.
The wheel turns
over bare decks,
shirts flap on a line;
only the song of the lapping waves
beats steady time…*

First mate,
off-duty from
the long dawn watch, begins
a letter to his wife, daydreams
of home.

The Captain's wife is late;
the child did not sleep
and breakfast has passed…
She, too, is missing home;
sits down at last to eat,
but can't quite force
the porridge down.
She swallows hard,
slices the top from her egg.

The second mate
is happy.
A four-hour sleep,
full stomach
and a quiet sea
are all he craves.
He has all three.

Shirts washed and hung, beds
made below, decks done, the boy
stitches a torn sail.

The Captain
has a good ear for a tune;
played his child to sleep
on the ship's organ.
Now, music left,
he checks his compass,
lightly tips the wheel,
hopes for a westerly.
Clear sky, a friendly sea,
fair winds for Italy.

The child now sleeps, at last,
head firmly pressed into her pillow
in a deep sea-dream.

Then why are the gulls wheeling
like vultures in the sky?
Why was the child snatched
from the sleep? What drew
the Captain's cry?

Only the wind replies
in the rigging,
and the hull creaks and sighs;
a sail spells out its message
over silent skies.
The wheel still turns
over bare decks,
shirts blow on the line;
the siren-song of lapping waves
still echoes over time.

Judith Nicholls

Unit two

Activity

The poet has **invented** details about the people on board – this helps us to picture them more easily.

- Choose three of the characters and write down four things you are told about them. Here is an example:

BOY
- he has done the washing
- he has made the beds
- he has cleaned the decks
- he is mending the sails.

The other characters are:

the Captain

his wife

his child

the first mate

the second mate

The cabin of the abandoned ship as it was found.

Activity

Read the first two verses again.

- List all the **sound** words in these verses, e.g. *sings, creaks.*
- Make another list of all the words suggesting **emptiness**, e.g. *vacant.*
- Make another list of all the words suggesting **peace** and **calm**, e.g. *lullaby.*

You will have picked out many words: this shows you how rich and descriptive the writing is. The poet, Judith Nicholls, has chosen her words very carefully.

Figurative language

Figurative language describes one thing in terms of another.

1. These people are described in terms of animals. Which animals?
   She hissed her goodbye.
   He scuttled to the door.
   He snorted with laughter.
   He truffled in a drawer.
   She squealed with delight.
   He bleated for his breakfast.

2. Find places in the poem where:

   - The ship is described in terms of a baby
   - The sea is described as a person
   - The sail is described in terms of something else – what?

3. Think of the rocking motion of a swing, and think up three things that you could compare it with, such as a ship rocking in the waves. Reread the first section of the *Mary Celeste* poem and write a poem called *Swing* in the same style.

The *Mary Celeste*

Unit two

Poems that tell a story

All these extracts are taken from poems that tell a story.

A
I went into the wood one day
And there I walked and lost my way
When it was so dark I could not see
A little creature came to me
He said if I would sing a song
The time would not be very long
But first I must let him hold my hand tight
Or else the wood would give me a fright
I sang a song, he let me go
But now I am home again there is nobody I know

B
'Is there anybody there?' said the Traveller,
Knocking on the moonlit door;
And his horse in the silence champed the grasses
Of the forest's ferny floor;
And a bird flew up out of the turret,
Above the Traveller's head;
And he smote upon the door again a second time;
'Is there anybody there?' he said.

C
Still it floundered forwards,
Still the city reeled;
There was panic on the pavements,
Even policemen squealed.
Then suddenly someone suggested
(As the beast had done no harm)
It would be kinder to show it kindness,
Better to stop the alarm.

D
It was many and many a year ago,
In a kingdom by the sea,
That a maiden there lived whom you may know
By the name of Annabel Lee;
And this maiden she lived with no other thought
Than to love and be loved by me.
I was a child and she was a child,
In this kingdom by the sea;
But we loved with a love that was more than love –
I and my Annabel Lee.

E
Sir Ralph the Rover tore his hair;
He cursed himself in his despair;
The waves rush in on every side,
The ship is sinking beneath the tide.
But even in his dying fear
One dreadful sound could the Rover hear
A sound as if with the Inchcape Bell
The Devil below was ringing his knell.

F
She has heard a whisper say,
A curse is on her if she stay
To look down to Camelot.
She knows not what the curse may be,
And so she weaveth steadily,
And little other care hath she,
The Lady of Shalott.

G
And when he came to his lady –
Looked over the castle wall –
He threw the head into her lap,
Saying 'Lady, take the ball!'
Says, 'Dost thou know thy Maurice' head,
When that thou dost it see?
Now lap it soft, and kiss it oft,
For thou loved'st him better than me.'

Try grouping the poems:
- By content – what they are about
- By central character – gender, class
- By setting – when and where the action takes place
- By narrator – what you can work out about the storyteller
- By interest – which ones make you want to read more.

What patterns do you notice?

> **HELP**
>
> Narrative poems are poems that tell a story. They were very popular during the 1800s. Most of them are about extraordinary events in the lives of ordinary people – death, love, crime, loss and ruin are very common themes. Many of them rhyme and almost all are written by men. Ballads tell stories in song.

Challenge

- Try putting the poems in order of age, with the oldest first.
- Try guessing which were written by men and which ones were written by women.

Answers on page 30.

Independent reading

Here are some narrative poems to read yourself:

A Speck Speaks by Adrian Mitchell
Ballad by Gerda Mayer
The Inchcape Rock by Robert Southey
Annabel Lee by Edgar Allan Poe
The Listeners by Walter de la Mare
Fairy Story by Stevie Smith
The Malfeasance by Alan Bold
Excelsior by Henry Wadsworth Longfellow

For each one:

- Stop half-way through and predict how it will end
- Give three clues you have used to make your prediction
- Stop just before the end and predict again
- At the end, consider how predictable the ending is, and how the writer prepared you for it.

For all of them:

- Make a list of five things that are common to most narrative poems.

Unit two

The Fire Dragon

Here is part of a very old poem called *Beowulf*.

Beowulf was a great warrior. As an old man he was asked by his people to help them fight the Fire Dragon. We have arranged this part of the text into six sections.

In the first section we meet the hero Beowulf in his armour. He is ready for battle. He is about to meet his enemy, the dragon.

Then the hero, stern under his gleaming helmet,
With his stout mailcoat and thick-plated shield,
Strode out to meet his foe. Toward the mound he moved,
The rock rampart cleft with arch of stone.

The second section describes how water in a stream is boiling because of the fire in the dragon's breath. The dragon has heated it up. The ground is so hot that Beowulf cannot walk on it.

                Close by,
Strongly from the earth gushed out a stream, whose wash,
Boiled to fury in the dragon's furnace breath,
Dropped to the steamy ground so scalding-fierce,
So hissing-hot that Beowulf could tread no farther.

In the third section, Beowulf wakes the dragon with a shout. The dragon is described waking up. Beowulf shouts that he will fight him!

He halted – in a loud voice he shouted his battle cry.
Then the dragon awoke. Crackling, he uncurled; like the clash
Of shield upon shield, he uncoiled his scaly length;
With thunder-clapping sound he twisted through the arch,
Spitting flame.

Unit two

The fourth section describes the dragon burning the grass as he stamps in rage on the ground.

>He blackened the rampart, he scorched
And burnt the grass, as round and round madly
He bounded upon the bruised ground.

The fifth section describes the start of the fight between the dragon and Beowulf. Beowulf hits the dragon, who gets very angry.

>Then Beowulf,
Wreathed in smoke and fire, ran upon the dragon;
Shielded, brandishing his sword, he struck him mightily –
The keen edge bit on the scales and glanced aside,
But roused his dreadful wrath.

The sixth section continues to describe the battle. The dragon eats up everything he can. Poor Beowulf ends up gasping for air.

> Uprearing, he flapped
> Wide his monstrous wings, fanning the blaze
> Tenfold; like a forest fire, tree-ravenous, devouring
> All in its path, he bore down on the pygmy king,
> Till Beowulf, choked in that frenzy of smoke and flame,
> Scarce could breathe . . . he stumbled . . . he gasped for air . . .
>
> From *Beowulf the Warrior* by Ian Serraillier

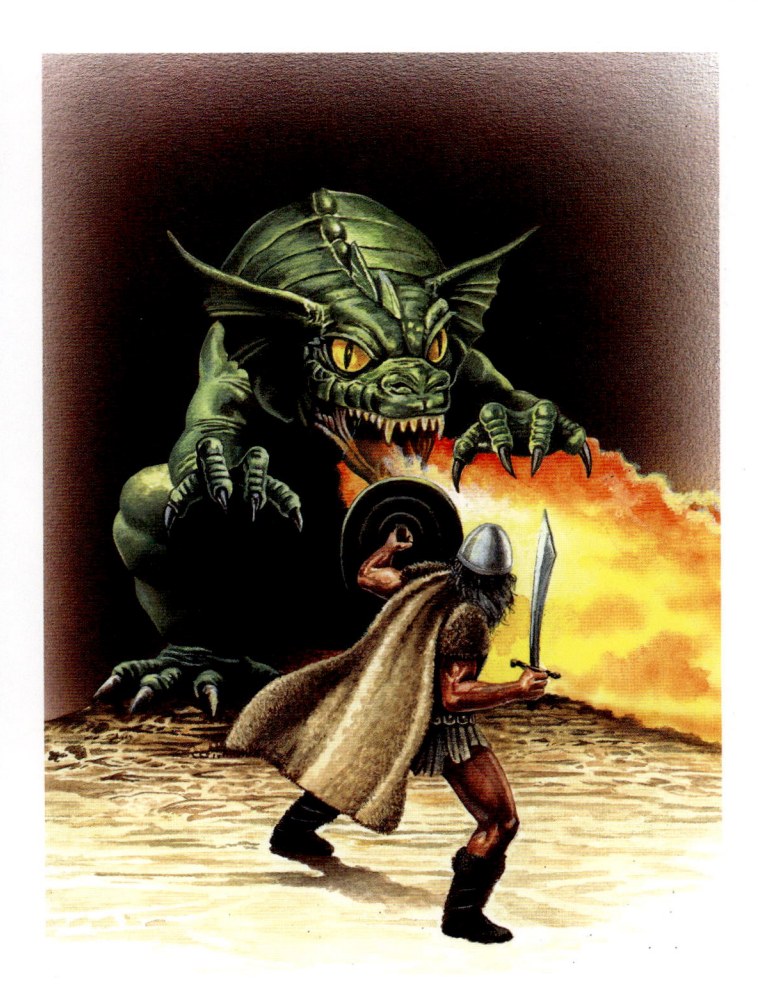

You are going to act out the fight between Beowulf and the Fire Dragon. These are sections three, four, five and six. Get into groups of four to six. One person is Beowulf, another is the dragon and the others are the readers.

Unit two

Activity

Instructions for the reading group

- Read your section as a group. Remember to stop at the punctuation marks!
- Slowly read your section and watch as Beowulf and the dragon act out what you are saying.
- Think carefully about how you read each part of your section. Read it in a way that sounds like the action it describes. Make it exciting for the listener.

Activity

Instructions for Beowulf and the Fire Dragon

- Read each section and decide what actions you will be doing in each section.
- As the group reads the section aloud, act out what they are saying. You may want to **freeze frame** a particular scene.

HELP

Freeze frame

Characters take up position as if a camera caught the act. Characters can be asked to speak aloud what they are thinking at that moment.

You have now acted out part of the story of Beowulf.
You have brought a poem to life!

ANSWERS TO PAGE 25

By age:
G *Childe Maurice* is traditional, passed on by word of mouth, and older than anyone can remember.
E *The Inchcape Rock* by Robert Southey
D *Annabel Lee* by Edgar Allan Poe
F *The Lady of Shalott* by Alfred Lord Tennyson
B *The Listeners* by Walter de la Mare
A *Fairy Story* by Stevie Smith
C *The Malfeasance* by Alan Bold

By gender:
Only *Fairy Story* is written by a woman.

UNIT THREE

Editor

The editor is the person who improves writing until it is good enough to print. In this unit, YOU are 'the editor'.

There are many good reasons for changing writing:

- To make it better
- To make it fit the space
- To make it like the rest
- To update it
- To correct it if it's wrong.

HELP

The editor uses symbols to tell the printer what needs changing.

Cut out	⊢⊣
Add in	⋏
Start a new paragraph	⌐
Change the order of letters	⊓⊔
Use capital letters	≡
Use bold	∼∼
Close the gap	⌒

The editor marks the text and writes any instructions in the margin.

Unit three

Task one: telling tales

You have to decide how you want the writer to tell the story.
Here is a page the writer has given you as a sample.

A NIGHT IN THE AIR RAID SHELTER

Thursday, 29 August 1940. He felt terrified and hid under his blanket. He was missing his mum and dad terribly. He heard the bombing carrying on all night. He could not sleep, and was cold, hungry and scared. He had a small box containing a gas mask. He clutched it to his chest and cried. When one particularly loud bomb went off he felt the shelter shake. 'That was a near one!' someone said in the darkness. Dust fell from the roof. He could feel it on his face and blanket. He dared not move. He would always remember that thunder of the bombs, the terrible noise hour after hour.

In the morning someone switched on the radio. The news announced that last night had seen the worst bombing up to now.

Who will tell the story?

The story is told in the **third person**. It tells us about the boy as if we were onlookers.

Try telling the story in the **first person**, as if you were the boy speaking as 'I'. Read it aloud slowly, changing the words as you go. What effect does it have?

Unit three

Writing in the first person can be more dramatic, and you feel close to the person who is 'I'. You only see what happens to 'I'. You live their story.

Sort these types of writing into first person and third person:

- Diary
- Biography
- Journal
- Autobiography
- Newspaper article
- Letter
- Factual information

Check your answers with the teacher.

> **HELP**
>
> **First person** – told from your own point of view as 'I'.
>
> **Third person** – told as an onlooker using 'he' or 'she'.

What tense to choose?

The story is told in the **past tense**. Find examples of at least five verbs written in the past tense.

Now try retelling the story in the **present tense** as if it is happening right now. Read it aloud slowly, changing the words as you go. What effect does it have?

> **HELP**
>
> **Using the present tense**
>
> Most stories are told in the past tense, as something that once happened and is now over. Sometimes stories are told in the present tense as if they are happening right now. It makes them very dramatic and you feel as if you are there. Other times to use the present tense are:
>
> - When describing something
> - When giving facts that are always true
> - When giving instructions or directions
> - When telling certain jokes
> - When saying how you feel.

Activity

Rewrite the passage so it is told in the first person and present tense, as if it is happening to you right now. Start: 'I feel terrified and hide under my blanket.'

Unit three

Task two: sexism

Another job for the editor is to check for sexism. It's unfair to make the boys always butch and the girls always giggly.

In this piece of writing, the woman has been caught looking through the man's books.

> She swung round, trembling, as she met Roland's black and angry stare. He took a stride towards her, and Christabel was terrified by what she saw in his face.
>
> Guilt made her stammer. 'I'm sorry, I was just . . .'
>
> 'Just what?' he snarled, reaching for the desk and snatching up a copy of one of his plays, holding it up for her to see, throwing it down again with a crash that made her jump. 'Prying?'
>
> His voice held a harsh note, his black brows were drawn.

Activity
- Find three typical butch things about Roland.
- Find three typical 'girly' things about Christabel.
- Find three words that tell you she was frightened.
- Find five words that tell you Roland was fierce.

Unit three

Acid test for sexism

Here's a way to check if something is sexist.
Try swapping the roles of the men and women.
Call Christabel Roland and call Roland Christabel.
Swap he and she, him and her.

Start: 'He swung round, trembling, as he met Christabel's black and angry stare. . .'

Could it ever happen? Is the passage sexist?

Boy or girl?

> I love dressing up and pretending to be other people, sometimes a ruby-lipped pirate, sometimes a beautiful princess.
>
> When I was three years old, my friend Georgina came round to my house to play with me and we both got dressed up in clothes from the dressing up box. I chose a pair of my mother's high-heeled shoes to complete my high fashion outfit. I felt so very grown up as I walked around the upstairs bedrooms in one of my mother's dresses and a pair of my mother's shoes. I was so happy with my best friend that I completely forgot I wasn't wearing my normal trainers.
>
> I took a step on to the stairs when BANG! I tripped and BUMP! BUMP! BUMP! I went all the way down to the bottom. OUCH!
>
> From *The Day I Wore High Heels* by Anna Cartwright

Activity

Write a similar episode from a boy's perspective. You might be rollerblading, learning to swim, stuck in a lift, or any one of a hundred catastrophes.

Unit three

Task three: from prose to picture

Your next job is to bring to life a comic strip that appears each week in your magazine for children. Brett Start is your hero – a hero of the 22nd century! Here is the last instalment:

Unit three

Next week's instalment: the storyline

Brett is locked in the Death Cell. It seems that nothing can save him. Evil Mastermind turns to the air pressure valve on the wall and slowly starts to turn it to start the timer that will release the poisonous gas. In ten minutes this will fill the cell with poison, killing the hero. 'In ten minutes' time you will be dead!' he sneers.

But Brett has spotted the keys hanging out of Mastermind's pocket. He has an idea!

Brett slides his leg quickly through the bars of the cell and kicks the keys out of Mastermind's pocket.

Mastermind is thrown off balance and Brett snatches the flying keys mid-air and unlocks the door from the inside.

Mastermind is back on his feet and a struggle ensues. Mastermind suddenly gets Brett in a neck lock over the bottomless Pit of Doom.

'Now I have you!' cries Mastermind. 'Your fate lies at the bottom of the bottomless Pit of Doom!'

It looks like Brett is bound to take a tumble!

More next week!

Activity

1. Draw six comic strip boxes and plan the second comic strip. A sketch will do.
   - Which parts were easy to change into pictures?
   - How did you choose which parts to leave out?
   - Find the parts that were hard to change into pictures. What made them hard?
2. Rewrite the first cartoon strip as an exciting part of a story.
   - Which parts are easy to change into prose?
   - Which parts don't convert easily and how do you make up for them?
3. Discuss the differences between prose and pictures:
   - What can pictures do that prose cannot?
   - What can prose do that pictures cannot?

Unit three

Task four: books on the box

Eagle TV have asked you to help them with a new programme called *Blockbuster Book*. The idea is to read a good book each night for a fortnight. Books are long and the programme lasts only half an hour. Instead of cutting parts out, they want to turn the books into plays. Your job is to decide if this is a good idea.

Here's a scene and its script from the first *Blockbuster Book*, *Buddy* by Nigel Hinton.

Novel

Buddy thought he was going to die when his dad came downstairs ready to go at six-thirty. He was dressed in his complete Teddy Boy outfit – drainpipe trousers, drape jacket with velvet collar, bootlace tie, thick crepe-soled shoes and fluorescent green socks. His hair was slicked back with oil and it was obvious that he'd taken great care to look as tidy as possible. He'd dressed himself in his 'best' for the occasion.

'I thought you had to go straight out afterwards,' Buddy said, not daring to come to the point but hoping his dad might change his mind and put on something else. Jeans – anything would be better than this.

'I am. Got me other stuff in 'ere,' he said, holding up a Woolworth's plastic bag. Buddy's stomach turned to water and he felt sick. The evening was going to be a disaster. 'Dad,' he said weakly.

'What?'

'Can't you put something else on?'

'Why?'

'Well, it's just…Mr Normington…won't like it.'

'He'll 'ave to lump it then, won't he?' There was defiance in his dad's voice but a touch of sadness, too, and Buddy knew he'd hurt him.

Playscript

Scene 11   *In Clarkes' hallway. Night.*

Buddy, neat, is standing at the bottom of the stairs. He checks his watch.

Buddy: Come on. It's nearly quarter to.

Terry: Keep your 'air on. I'm coming.

Terry comes down the stairs in full Teddy Boy outfit. It is the first time we have seen him in the full regalia. He is carrying a plastic bag.

Buddy: I thought you had to go straight to work after.

Terry: I 'ave. Got me other stuff in 'ere.

Buddy: Dad.

Terry: What?

Buddy: Can you put something else on?

Terry: It's me best.

Buddy: I know but…Mr Normington…won't like it.

Terry: He'll 'ave to lump it then, won't he?

Terry goes defiantly to the door and opens it.

Terry: Well?
Buddy follows. The door closes.

Fill in a grid to list the differences between the prose and the script:

In the prose	In the script	Why the difference?

Eagle TV decide they don't like the idea, but Radio Eagle does. They think they can use the script to read aloud. You aren't so sure. In a group:

- Read the script aloud.
- What difficulties would it pose for radio listeners?
- Can you see any ways of getting round the difficulties?
- Rewrite the script for radio.

EagleInternetBooks.com is considering putting new books on the internet, and readers pay them for the time spent logged on to read. They ask you for your opinion. List the advantages and disadvantages and any other important points to make, like this:

Advantages	Disadvantages	Other points to consider

Unit three

Unit three

Task five: cutting down

Your next job is to edit down two pages of writing.

The writing is good but there's only room for one page of text. You have to decide how to edit it.

> **HELP**
>
> **How to reduce the text:**
> - Cut out some of the items
> - Cut out the details
> - Shrink the size of print or pictures
> - Change the presentation, e.g. to bullet points
> - Combine any of these
>
> **What to cut out:**
> - The least interesting parts
> - The least important parts
> - The parts that stand alone and won't be missed

In pairs, edit down the two pages opposite to one page. Discuss the advantages and disadvantages of different ways of doing this.

A similar job has to be done for a poster that gives information about the top ten chart hits:

THIS WEEK'S TOP TEN	
No. 1	No. 2
No. 3	No. 4
No. 5	No. 6
No. 7	No. 8
No. 9	No. 10

The poster has to be edited down to half its size. Suggest five different ways of doing this, and provide a new title for each section.

'Giverny is splendid'

In 1883, Monet moved his family to Giverny which is a village north-west of Paris. The house at Giverny was to be his home until he died 37 years later. It was a long building, painted pink on the outside and two storeys high. It was big enough to take Monet's large family in comfort.

While Monet lived at Argenteuil, he had become an enthusiastic gardener and had a great interest in different kinds of plants and flowers. The house at Giverny had a very large garden and Monet soon set about rearranging it.

The Water-Lily Pond and the Japanese Bridge, 1899 ➤
Monet built a Japanese bridge over the small lake in his garden. He planted wisteria to grow over the bridge and water-lilies in the lake. In 1899, he began a series of paintings of the bridge. This painting shows the bridge on a summer afternoon.

■ *The first thing you see in this picture is the strong curve of the bridge and this leads you to look at the water-lilies below. Monet left out the sky on purpose because it would take your eye away from the bridge and the pond.*

▲ **The House at Giverny**
This was a comfortable family home surrounded by a large garden. At first, Monet rented but later he could afford to buy it.

◀ **The Yellow Dining Room**
The dining room at Giverny is kept as it was in Monet's time. Here the family would eat lunch at midday and supper at about 7.30 in the evening.

The household was organised around Monet's needs. He got up early in the morning, had a cold bath and breakfast. Then he went out to paint until lunchtime and went out painting again in the afternoon until supper time. He usually went to bed at 9.30 pm so that he could get up early the next day.

The children often went out with him and helped to carry his canvases, easel and paints. If the weather was wet Monet was very bad-tempered and sometimes stayed in bed all day.

▼ **The Flat-Bottomed Boat**
A copy of Monet's flat-bottomed rowing boat is still used to clear the water weed that grows in the lily pond at Giverny. This kind of boat is known as a Norwegian.

Unit three

Unit three

Task six: selling it like it is

Your last task is to write advertising for three products no one wants to buy.

- A slimy green nail polish that won't set

- A sweet that makes you burp again and again

- A mobile phone with no battery; it dies after 10 hours of use

1. Find three good selling points for each product.
2. Think up a great name for each.
3. Sum it up in a catchy jingle or rhyme.
4. Write **either** a script for a radio advertisement **or** a script for a television commercial **or** design a poster.

UNIT FOUR

The Ice Maiden

In this unit you will read a short story by a well-known author. You will discover how the story works.

Meet Paul Jennings

Paul Jennings' road to fame began in 1985 with the publication of *Unreal!* This collection of gripping short stories quickly reached the bestseller lists. It has been eagerly devoured by hungry young readers. Every new book written since *Unreal!* has been met with widespread acclaim. The stories are funny, quirky, zany and yucky, and have wonderful surprise endings. The stories are enjoyed by readers of all ages. Paul Jennings has won a wide range of awards. In 1990, a thirteen-part TV series was screened in Australia and in the UK. The series, *Round the Twist*, quickly became the top-rating children's programme. Paul Jennings has written over eighty stories so far.

The reason that Paul Jennings' books are so popular is that he hasn't forgotten what it feels like to be young. 'I can remember all the fears and feelings of childhood that aren't so good. Feeling very small and powerless. The guilt and the embarrassment. The monster that I was quite sure lurked in the shadows. These are the things that I write about in my stories and which make some children ask, "How do you know what it's like to be me?" '

To find out more about Paul Jennings, go to his website at: www.pauljennings.com.au/

Unit four

> **Activity**
> Can you find any of the titles on these two pages in your school/local library?

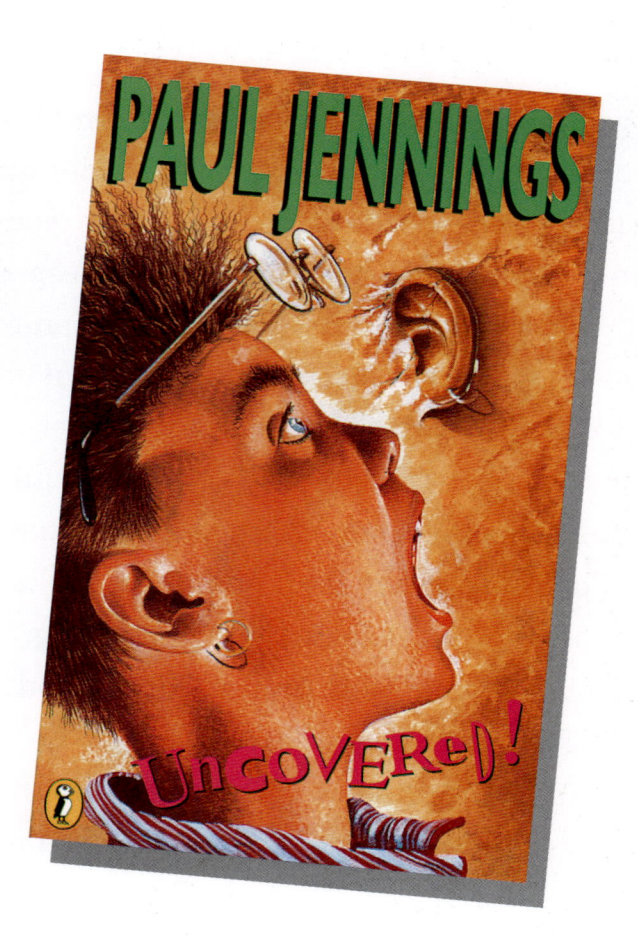

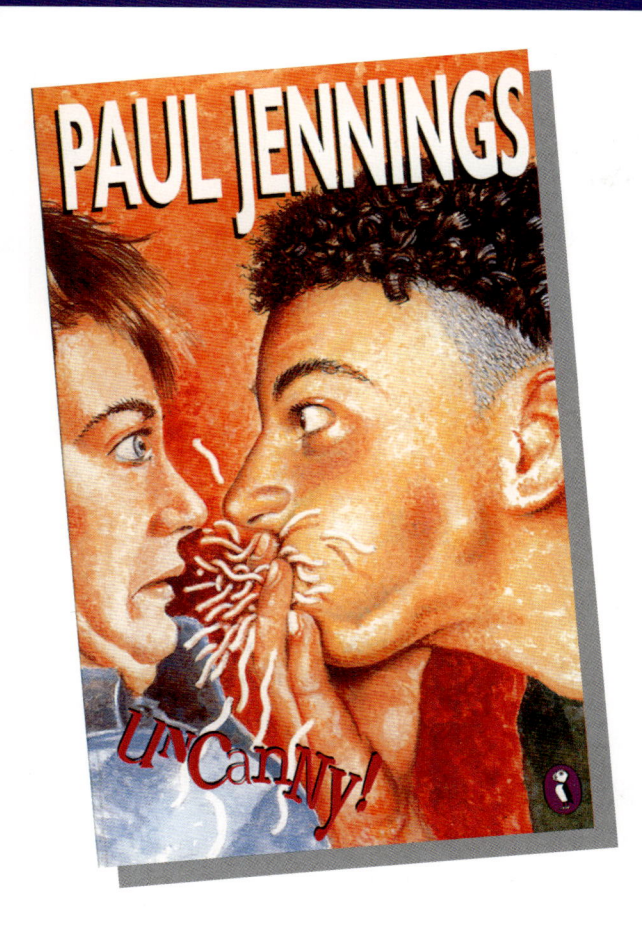

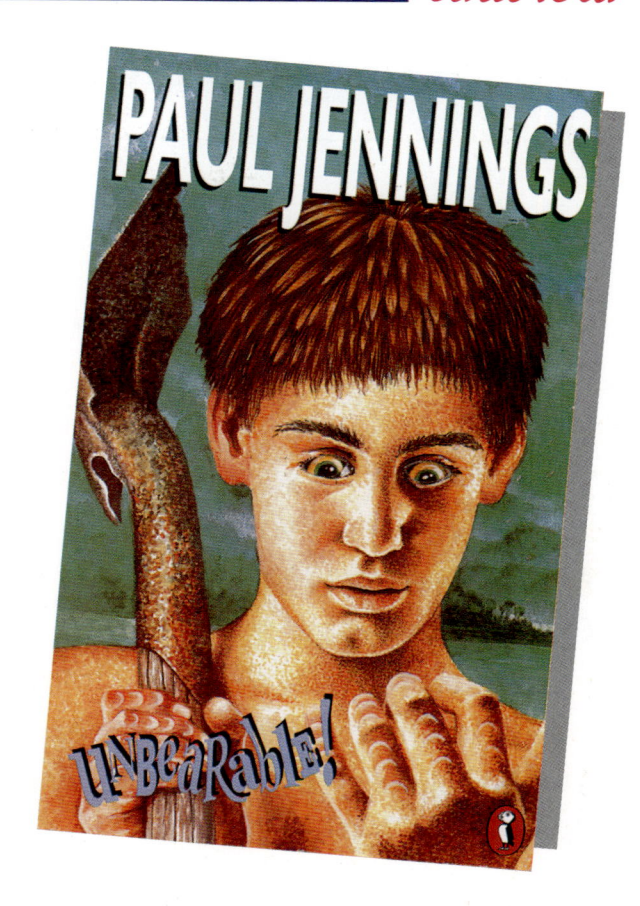

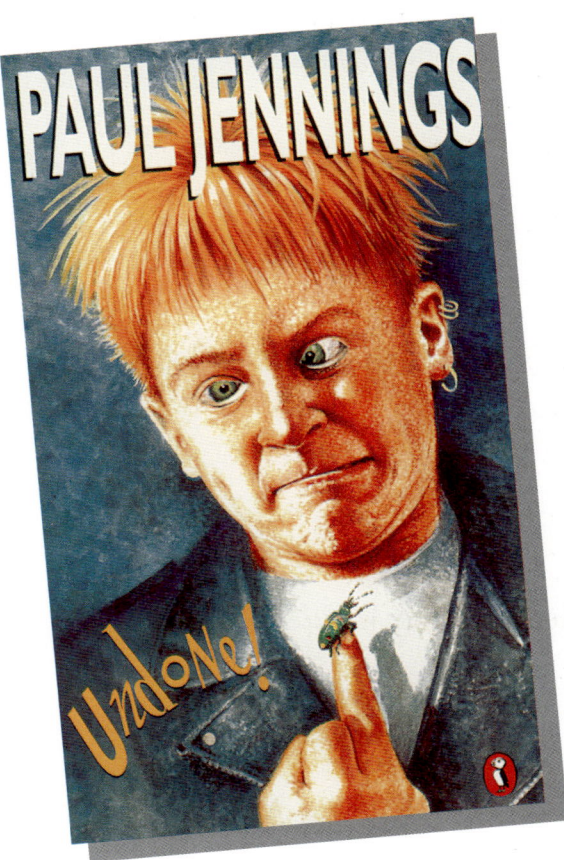

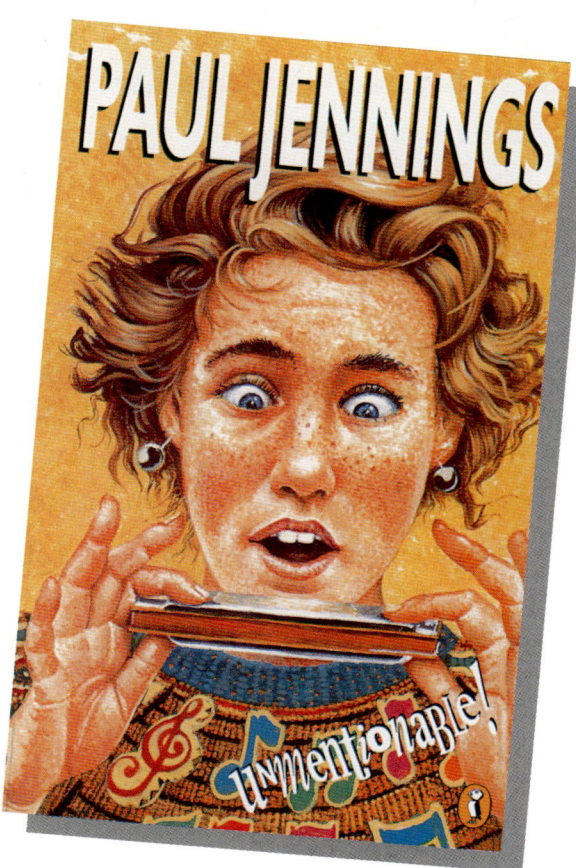

Unit four

Unit four

A taste of the writer's style

> ### Activity
>
> Read these first sentences. They come from different stories by Paul Jennings. Then discuss the questions in pairs.
>
> **'Okay, I shouldn't have done it. I was stupid.'**
> (Extract from *Cry Baby*)
> - What do you think this person has done?
> - What kind of story are you expecting?
> - How might the story develop from this point?
>
> **'Mr Simpkin decided to run away from home.'**
> (Extract from the *Velvet Throne*)
> - Do adults normally 'run away from home'?
> - What might Mr Simpkin be escaping from?
>
> **'The people are so far below they look like little pins.'**
> (Extract from *Eyes Knows*)
> - Where is this person?
> - How could this person have found him/herself in this position?
>
> **'Sean flapped his wings nervously.'**
> (Extract from *Birdman*)
> - Why has Sean got wings?
> - What could make him nervous?

You have looked at first sentences from a range of Paul Jennings stories.
You have looked at the front covers of his books.

- What kind of writer do you think he is?
- What do you expect to find in his stories?

Now read this story by Paul Jennings. It is called *The Ice Maiden*.

The Ice Maiden

Section one

I just wouldn't go anywhere near a redhead.

Now don't get me wrong and start calling me a hairist or something like that. Listen to what I have to say, then make up your mind.

It all started with Mr Mantolini and his sculptures.

They were terrific, were Mr Mantolini's frozen statues. He carved them out of ice and stood them in the window of his fish shop which was over the road from the pier. A new ice carving every month.

Sometimes it would be a beautiful peacock with its tail fanned out. Or maybe a giant fish thrashing itself to death on the end of a line. One of my favourites was a kangaroo with a little joey peering out of her pouch.

Unit four

It was a bit sad really. On the first day of every month Mr Mantolini would throw the old statue out the back into an alley. Where it would melt and trickle away into a damp patch on the ground.

A new statue would be in the shop window. Sparkling blue and silver as if it had been carved from a solid chunk of the Antarctic shelf.

Every morning on my way to school, I would stop and stare at his statue. And on the first of every month I would be there after school to see the new one.

I couldn't bear to go around the back and watch yesterday's sculpture melt into the mud.

'Why do you throw them out?' I asked one day.

Mr Mantolini shrugged. 'You live. You die,' he said.

Mr Mantolini took a deep breath. Now he was going to ask me something. The same old thing he had asked every day for weeks.

Unit four

'My cousin Tony come from Italy. Next month. You take to school. You friend. My cousin have red hair. You like?'

I gave him my usual answer. 'Sorry,' I said, 'I won't be able to.' I couldn't tell him that it was because I hated red hair. I didn't want to hurt his feelings.

He just stood there without saying anything. He was disappointed in me because we were friends. He knew how much I liked his ice statues and he always came out to talk to me about them. 'You funny boy,' he said. He shook his head and walked inside.

I thought I saw tears in Mr Mantolini's eyes. I knew I had done the wrong thing again. And I was sorry. But I didn't want a redhead for a mate.

Activity

Discuss in pairs:
- What do you think the boy has got against redheads?
- Do you think this is a good beginning to the story?

On your own:
- Copy the grid below. Make two lists of everything you learn about:
  a) Mr Mantolini
  b) the **narrator**.

Mr Mantolini	The narrator
Comes from Italy	Hates redheads
Runs a fish shop	Lives near the sea

★ Glossary

The **narrator** is the voice of the story. The author, Paul Jennings, is telling the story as if he is a teenage boy. The teenage boy is the narrator.

Unit four

Section two

I felt guilty and miserable all day. But after school I cheered up a bit. It was the first of September. There would be a new ice statue in the window. It was always something to look forward to.

I hurried up to the fish shop and stared through the glass. I couldn't believe what I saw. The ice statue was of a girl. It reminded me of one of those Greek sculptures that you see in museums. It had long tangled hair. And smiling lips. Its eyes sparkled like frozen diamonds. I tell you this. That ice girl was something else. She was fantastic.

'You're beautiful,' I said under my breath. 'Beautiful.'

Of course she was only a statue. She couldn't see or hear me. She was just a life-sized ice maiden, standing among the dead fish in the shop window. She was inside a glass fridge which kept her cold. Her cheeks were covered with frost.

I stood there for ages just gawking at her. I know it was stupid. I would have died if anyone knew what I was thinking. How embarrassing. I had a crush on a piece of ice.

Every day after that, I visited the fish shop. I was late for school because of the ice maiden. I filled every spare minute of my time standing outside the window. It was as if I was hypnotised. The ice maiden's smile seemed to be made just for me.

'Get real,' I said to myself. 'What are you doing here? You fool.'

I knew I was mad but something kept drawing me back to the shop.

Mr Mantolini wouldn't meet my gaze. He was cross with me.

I pretended the ice girl was my friend. I told her my secrets. Even though she was made of ice, I had this silly feeling that she understood.

Mr Mantolini saw me watching her. But he didn't come outside. And whenever I went inside to buy fish for Mum, he scurried out the back and sent his assistant to serve me.

Activity

- What is the boy thinking about when he looks at the statue?
- Paul Jennings has used a range of adjectives to show how much the boy admires the ice maiden. Make a list of the adjectives used to describe the boy's reaction to the ice maiden.
- Write a short diary entry for the boy on this day. Record his thoughts and feelings about the ice maiden.

Unit four

Section three

The days passed. Weeks went by. The ice maiden smiled on and on. She never changed. The boys thought I was nuts standing there gawking at a lump of ice. But she had this power over me – really. Kids started to tease me. 'He's in love,' said a girl called Simone. I copped a lot of teasing at school but still I kept gazing in that window.

As the days went by I grew sadder and sadder. I wanted to take the ice girl home. I wanted to keep her for ever. But once she was out of her glass cage, in the warm air, her smiling face would melt and drip away.

I dreaded the first of October. When Mr Mantolini would take the ice maiden and dump her in the alley. To be destroyed by the warm rays of the sun.

On the last day of September I waited until Mr Mantolini was serving in the shop. 'You can't throw her out,' I yelled. 'She's too lovely. She's real. You mustn't. You can't.' I was nearly going to say, 'I love her,' but that would have been stupid.

Mr Mantolini looked at me and shrugged. 'You live. You die,' he said. 'She ice. She cold. She water.'

I knew it was no good. Tomorrow Mr Mantolini would cast the ice girl out into the alley.

The next day I wagged school. I hid in the alley and waited. The minutes dragged their feet. The hours seemed to crawl. But then, as I knew he would, Mr Mantolini emerged with the ice maiden. He dumped her down by the rubbish bins. Her last resting place was to be among the rotting fish heads in an empty alley.

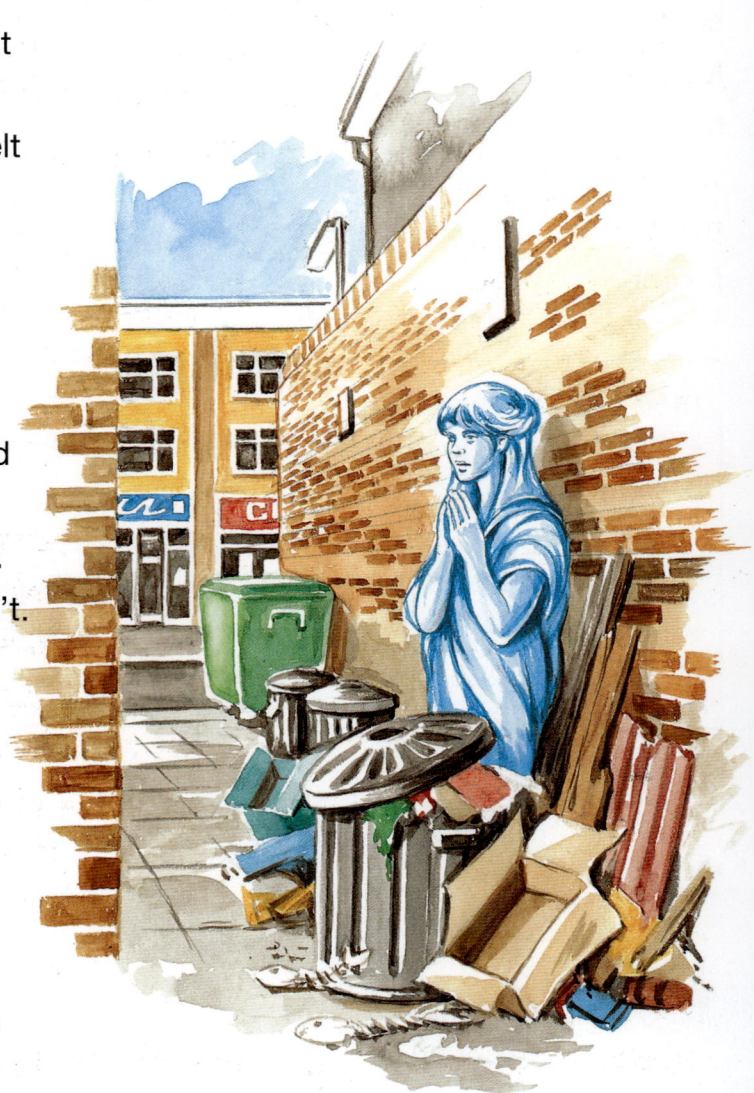

Unit four

Mr Mantolini disappeared back into the shop. I rushed over to my ice maiden. She was still covered in frost and had sticky, frozen skin.

My plan was to take her to the butcher. I would pay him to keep the ice maiden in his freezer where I could visit her every day. I hadn't asked him yet. But he couldn't say no, could he?

The sun was rising in the sky. I had to hurry.

The ice maiden still stooped. She seemed to know that her time had come. 'Don't worry,' I said. 'I'll save you.'

I don't know what came over me. I did something crazy. I bent down and gently kissed her on the mouth.

Activity

- Which lines in Section three tell us about Mr Mantolini's views on life and love?
- Read Section three again carefully with a partner. Look at the conversation between the boy and Mr Mantolini. Try acting out this scene to show:
    1. How obsessed the boy has become about the ice maiden.
    2. How unconcerned or casual Mr Mantolini appears. You could even try out an Italian accent!
- You could extend this activity to include the 'hidden emotions'. This means that you need another person to say aloud what the boy and Mr Mantolini are really thinking while they are speaking.

HELP

You could prepare this scene as a playscript. This means writing out the speech so that it can be performed.

Stage directions

For example:

Boy: *(shouts in angry, disbelieving voice)*
You can't throw her out!

In your stage directions you will need to think about:

- How to emphasise lines of speech
- What movements and facial expressions are needed to bring across how the boy and Mr Mantolini feel.

Unit four

Section four

It was a long kiss. The longest kiss ever in the history of the world. My lips stuck to hers. My flesh froze on to the ice. Cold needles of pain numbed my lips. I tried to pull away but I couldn't. The pain made my eyes water. Tears streamed down my face and across the ice maiden's cheeks.

On we kissed. And on. And on. I wanted to pull my mouth away but much as I cared for the ice girl, I didn't want my lips to tear away, leaving bleeding skin as a painful reminder of my madness. There I was, kissing ice lips, unable to move.

I tried to yell for help but I couldn't speak. Muffled grunts came out of my nose. Horrible nasal noises. No one came to help me. The alley echoed with the noise. I grabbed the ice maiden and lifted her up. She was heavy. Her body was still sticky with frost. My fingers stuck fast. She was my prisoner. And I was hers.

The sun warmed my back. Tears of agony filled my eyes. If I waited there she would melt. I would be free but the ice maiden would be gone. Her lovely nose and chin would drip away to nothing.

Unit four

But the cold touch of the ice girl was terrible. Her smiling lips burnt my flesh. The tip of my nose was frozen. I ran out of the alley into the street. There was a group of people waiting by a bus-stop near the end of the pier. 'Help, get me unstuck. But don't hurt the ice maiden,' was what I tried to say.

But what came out was, 'Nmn nnmmm nnnn nng ng ng mn nm.'

The people looked at me as if I was crazy. Some of them laughed. They thought I was acting the fool. An idiot pretending to kiss a statue.

I ran over to Mr Mantolini's shop and tried to knock on the window with my foot. I had to balance on one leg, while holding the ice girl in my arms and painfully kissing her at the same time. I fell over with a crunch. Oh agony, oh misery, oh pain. My lips, my fingers, my knees.

There was no sign of Mr Mantolini. He must have been in the back room.

Unit four

Activity

- What have you learned so far about the person telling the story? List five pieces of evidence from the text in a grid like the one below. The first one has been done for you.

What I found	What it tells me
1. *'That ice girl was something else. She was fantastic.'*	The boy found the statue very attractive and special.
2.	
3.	
4.	
5.	

What will happen next?

On the opposite page are six cards for you to copy and cut out.
Underneath the pictures are captions.

Activity

- Put cards A to D in the right order. Then do your own picture and caption for E and F.

Unit four

A

'That ice girl was something else. She was fantastic.'

B

'My cousin Tony come from Italy. Next month. You take to school. You friend. My cousin have red hair. You like?'

C

'She was my prisoner. And I was hers.'

D

'"He's in love," said a girl called Simone.'

E

F

You can read the rest of the story at the end of this unit.

Unit four

A look at love

The Ice Maiden is a story about a powerful 'first love' experience. Read the following poem, which describes another first meeting.

First Love

I ne'er was struck before that hour
With love so sudden and so sweet,
Her face it bloomed like a sweet flower
And stole my heart away complete.
My face turned pale as deadly pale,
My legs refused to walk away,
And when she looked 'what could I ail?'
My life and all seemed turned to clay.

And then my blood rushed to my face
And took my sight away.
The trees and bushes round the place
Seemed midnight at noonday.
I could not see a single thing,
Words from my eyes did start;
They spoke as chords do from the string,
And blood burnt round my heart.

Are flowers the winter's choice?
Is love's bed always snow?
She seemed to hear my silent voice
And love's appeal to know.

I never saw so sweet a face
As that I stood before;
My heart has left its dwelling-place
And can return no more.

John Clare (1793–1864)

Unit four

Activity

In a group:

- Go through the poem verse by verse. Make a list of the 'loving' words and phrases used by the poet to describe his 'new love'.
- 'Her face it bloomed like a sweet flower' is an example of a **simile**. Can you see other similes in this poem? What do they describe?

On your own:

- List all the words, phrases and expressions that tell the reader this is not a modern poem.
- Describe the physical changes that overcome this person after he falls in love. Write down the words in the text to help you complete this task. For example:

  'My face turned pale…'

- How do you think this person feels?

59

Unit four

Objects can be used as symbols or signs of love. People often give gifts as a sign of their love. Read the following poem, 'Valentine'. A 'valentine' is a symbol of love.

Valentine

Not a red rose or a satin heart

I give you an onion.
It is a moon wrapped in brown paper.
It promises light
Like the careful undressing of love.

Here.
It will blind you with tears
Like a lover.
It will make your reflection
A wobbling photo of grief.

I am trying to be truthful.

Not a cute card or a kissogram.

I give you an onion.
Its fierce kiss will stay on your lips,
Possessive and faithful
As we are,
For as long as we are.

Take it.
Its platinum loops shrink to
a wedding-ring,
If you like.

Lethal.
Its scent will cling to your fingers,
Cling to your knife.

Carol Ann Duffy

Activity

Work in pairs.

- Take turns to read the poem on page 60, to each other as if you were giving each other the valentine gift.
- What words or phrases does the poet use to describe the onion?
- Make a list of the things that the poet says the onion promises or does.
- Why do you think the poet has used the onion as a symbol of love? Does it make love sound like a happy feeling?
- What words or phrases does the poet use to show love might be a difficult feeling?

Now work on your own.

- Read 'First Love' on page 58 and 'Valentine' on page 60. Use the following points to help you write two paragraphs comparing the two poems.
  - Content and ideas: what are the poems about?
  - The language the poets use: is it formal or informal and 'chatty'?
  - Structure: do the poets use verse? Is there a rhyme scheme?
  - Language features: what images do the poets create?
  - Your personal response: what do you like or dislike about each poem?

Unit four

The Ice Maiden (concluded)

Section five

What could I do? I looked out to sea. If I jumped into the water it would melt the ice. My lips and fingers would come free. But the ice maiden would melt. 'Let me go,' I whispered in my mind. She made no answer.

My hands were numb. Cold pins pricked me without mercy. I ran towards the pier. I spoke to my ice maiden again, without words. 'I'm sorry. I'm sorry, sorry, sorry.'

I jogged along the pier. Further and further. My feet drummed in time with my thoughts. 'Sorry, sorry, sorry.'

I stopped and stared down at the waves. Then I closed my eyes and jumped, still clutching the ice-cold girl to my chest. Down, I plunged. For a frozen moment I hung above the ocean. And then, with a gurgle and a groan, I took the ice lady to her doom.

The waves tossed above us. The warm water parted our lips. My fingers slipped from her side. I bobbed up like an empty bottle and saw her floating away. Already her eyes had gone. Her hair was a glassy mat. The smiling maiden smiled no more. She was just a lump of ice melting in the waves.

'No,' I screamed. My mouth filled with salt water and I sank under the sea.

They say that your past life flashes by you when you are drowning. Well, it's true. I re-lived some horrible moments. I remembered the time in a small country school when I was just a little kid. And the only redhead. I saw the school bully Johnson teasing me every day. Once again I sat on the school bench at lunch-time – alone and rejected. Not allowed to hang around with the others. Just because Johnson didn't like red hair. Once again I could hear him calling me 'carrots' and 'ginger'. They were the last thoughts that came to me before the world vanished into salty blackness.

Unit four

Unit four

Section six

But I didn't drown. In a way my hair saved me. It must have been easy for them to spot my curly locks swirling like red seaweed thrown up from the ocean bed.

Mr Mantolini pulled me out. He and his cousin. I could hear him talking even though I was only half conscious. 'You live. But you not die yet.'

I didn't want to open my eyes. I couldn't bear to think about what I had done to the ice maiden. I was alive but she was dead. Gone for ever.

In the end I looked up. I stared at my rescuers. Mr Mantolini and his cousin.

She had red tangled hair. And smiling lips. Her eyes sparkled like frozen diamonds. I tell you this. That girl Tony was something else. She was fantastic.

'You're beautiful,' I said under my breath. 'Beautiful.'

Mr Mantolini's ice statue had been good. But not as good as the real thing. After all, it had only been a copy of his cousin Tony. I smiled up at her. And she smiled back. With a real smile.

I guess that's when I discovered that an ice maiden who is dead is not sad. And a nice maiden who is red, is not bad.

Not bad at all.

Inventive endings

> ### Activity
>
> Read the end of the story again:
>
> 'I guess that's when I discovered that an ice maiden who is dead is not sad. And a nice maiden who is red, is not bad. Not bad at all.'
>
> - What makes this a good ending? Look closely at the words Paul Jennings has used.
> - Did the story end in the way you expected? What does Paul Jennings do to make a surprise ending?

Unit four

Now you have read *The Ice Maiden*, you can work through the following activities.

Using drama

Activity

Work in pairs. Take it in turns to go into role as the boy and Mr Mantolini.

1. Devise a set of questions to ask each character and refer closely to developments in the story to help you.

Here are some examples of opening questions:

- What is your name?
- Do you have any strong likes/dislikes?
- Have you always lived in this country?
- Do you enjoy your job?

2. When you have devised your questions you can 'go into role' as each character.

Activity

Work in small groups.

1. On a copy of page 66, complete the storyboard. Add captions and draw the scene the caption describes. Choose key moments in the story.
2. You are going to prepare a **freeze frame** of key moments in the story. Use the storyboard to help you plan your freeze frame. Choose the three frames that you like best. Present them to the rest of the class.

HELP

Freeze frame

This means you act out key moments in the story. You then 'freeze' the story as if a camera caught the act.

Unit four

1. 'They were terrific, were Mr Mantolini's frozen statues.'

2.

3.

4. 'I grabbed the ice maiden and lifted her up.'

5.

6.

Unit four

Writing a review

You have read the complete text of *The Ice Maiden* and know a lot about how the story was written. Now you need to show what you know and understand by writing a short review of the story.

A 'review' is a piece of writing that allows you to give your views and opinion of the story. It is designed to help other readers decide whether to read the text for themselves. So you don't want to give too much of the story away.

Activity

1. Decide on five key points you want to make about the story. For example:
   - Some details about the author
   - A short summary of the basic idea of the story without telling it all
   - The 'style' of the story. Paul Jennings has a distinctive style. Find some good examples and explain why they are effective
   - Say something about the surprise ending (without giving the game away)
   - Finish with a paragraph in which you give your views on how successful a story *The Ice Maiden* is and why you think this.

2. Now write a short paragraph for each point. Each paragraph should contain at least three or four sentences. Use some of these paragraph starters to help you:
   - Paul Jennings is . . .
   - In *The Ice Maiden*, the writer introduces us to . . .
   - The story is told by a narrator who . . .
   - You can easily recognise a story by Paul Jennings. He . . .
   - Many of Paul Jennings' stories have surprise endings. Here, . .
   - Overall, I think the story is . . .

3. Make sure you include at least three short quotations as evidence for the points you are making, especially in the third paragraph.

HELP

Using quotations

- Make the point you want to make, e.g. *Paul Jennings writes in the first person to show how a teenage boy thinks*.

- Then use a short quotation from the text as evidence: *'The boys thought I was nuts standing there gawking at a lump of ice.'*

- Put the two together using a colon and quotation marks: *Paul Jennings writes in the first person to show how a teenage boy thinks: 'The boys thought I was nuts standing there gawking at a lump of ice.'*

UNIT FIVE

Smart Reading

Little Brother

The Latest Reality TV Game Show!
(Designed specifically for schools.)

Task 1: What's all this about?

Find out quickly by using the first skill: skimming

Skills check: Skimming

Skimming is a skill you use to get a quick idea of what a passage is all about. To skim this page, you will need to cast your eyes rapidly over the page and locate only the essential information.

Direct your own 'Little Brother' show for charity in your school! Here's how:

- Choose the best five contestants (pupils from your school) to go into the Little Brother house (the media studies room) for just one day.
- Use a VCR to beam the pictures on to a television screen in the school hall.
- Organise a range of competitions and activities for the participants such as: quizzes, in-depth discussions, making papier-mâché masks, etc.
- Place a separate VCR in a suitable place for a video diary.
- At the end of the day, ask pupils and staff to pay £1 to vote for the best contestant who will win a special prize decided by the organisers.

Unit five

LITTLE BROTHER RULES

- Five contestants will remain in the Little Brother house for one day.
- Nothing can be taken into the Little Brother house.
- Contestants will be filmed continuously throughout the day.
- Tasks will be set throughout the day to win food.
- At the end of the day voters will decide on the winner.

Invitation

The directors of 'Little Brother' (actually a group of teachers at your school) challenge you to organise this charity event for the school by:

◆

Agreeing to the challenge of being the Little Brother project manager (working on your own or with a small group)

◆

Carefully reviewing the ten candidates for inclusion

◆

Choosing five contestants from the list available on the following pages

◆

Preparing a submission to the directors to explain your final choices.

REPLY:

Thank you for your kind invitation. I would be delighted to accept because . . .

....

Unit five

The terrific ten

Task 2: Who wants to be in?

Read through the following mini-biographies to get an idea of the sort of pupils who have applied to be in the Little Brother house. You will eventually have to make the decision about who to leave out, but for now, just get to know them.

> **Skills check: Scanning**
>
> This reading skill is similar to skimming except that you start to read a little more carefully. Take a little more time, read through the details of the ten candidates and see if you can pick out some important features which will help you decide.

Tania: My name is Tania and I'm the outdoors type. I love walking, any form of team sports (although I'm not that good at them) and being in the Guides. I really enjoy meeting new people and talking to them; maybe it's because I come from a large family. I also have a dog called D-fer ('D' for dog, get it?) and I would love for him to be in the Little Brother house too.

David: Hi! I'm David and I enjoy a good laugh with my mates and I really like watching sport on the telly – usually football. I play in goal for the school team and I used to be a member of the Scouts for a short time. I have one brother and one sister and I want to be included because it would be really cool.

Sarah: After a lot of thought, I finally plucked up the courage to apply (mainly because my older brother, Joe, told me to) and I think I'd enjoy it. Most of the time I enjoy reading books and I love travelling whenever I can. I want to be in the house because it would help me to overcome my shyness and to get on with other people.

Iaz: Most people say that I'm a very determined person and I'd have to agree. I love to win at anything really – sport, games, debates . . . anything. My hobbies include mountain biking and computer games and I want to be in the Little Brother house because I believe I can win.

Unit five

Safina: My friends tell me they like me because I listen and give them good advice when they have a problem. I think I'm lucky because I make friends easily and I do love to talk. I come from a family of five – me, my parents and my two older sisters – and we all get on really well. I want to be in the show because I want to raise lots of money for charity.

Gareth: My name is Gareth and I have a wide range of interests from reading to sport. I enjoy playing team sports like football and cricket and I also like to get involved in debates and discussions. I have a few close friends and I enjoy having a laugh with them as well as reading books and comics and watching TV. I want to be in the Little Brother house because I think it would be a really interesting experience.

Suzi: As an only child, I suppose you would say that I'm a quiet person but I do enjoy being with other people. I absolutely love reading (my favourite author is Philip Pullman) and I also enjoy doing tapestry, which I learnt from my mother. I would like to be included because I would like the money raised to go to a charity for the homeless.

Peter: My interests include painting, watching cartoons, reading books and riding my bike. I also really enjoy discussions on all sorts of topics and I want to get into Little Brother because I'd like the money to go to animal welfare.

Avril: I guess you'd call me outgoing because I like speaking my mind. My friends say that I have a bubbly personality and I like to go out and have fun when I'm not doing my homework. I have a wide circle of friends and enjoy a quiet chat or a heated argument – whatever's happening, I suppose. I just love to be involved. I do like reading and I'm told that I'm also a good listener. I want to be in Little Brother because it will be really good fun.

Ahmed: I'm outgoing and I have lots of friends. I enjoy music (I play in a band) and I spend time (too much time my mum says) on the computer. In the future, I want to be a journalist so that I can ask lots of difficult questions. I suppose I want to be in Little Brother so that I can become famous (well, in school anyway).

Unit five

Task 3: Finding the 'meat'

Your task in this section is to begin to look more closely at the candidates. The TV directors have e-mailed you with some helpful suggestions. You will need to read back through the applications to locate some evidence.

> **Skills check: Scanning**
>
> In this activity, you will be scanning to locate information. One way of doing this is to run your fingers quickly over the text (faster than you would normally read) to find what you are looking for.

E-mail:
The TV directors want you to be very careful selecting the contestants for Little Brother. Apparently, the headteacher and the governors are a bit concerned. Read the 'Guidelines' (below) and then look back to the mini-biographies to get your evidence. (An example has been done for you.)

Guidelines (No. 1)

We want the final five contestants to be confident, outgoing personalities so that they do not get too embarrassed being 'televised'.

Confident, outgoing candidates	Evidence
• Ahmed	• Outgoing, lots of friends, plays in a band
•	•
•	•

73

© HODDER MURRAY   *Checkpoint English 2*

Unit five

Guidelines (No. 2)

Remember, team games are an important part of the day's activities. Who are the people who are best able to contribute positively to a team?

Team players	Evidence:
• Gareth	• Enjoys playing a number of team sports
•	•
•	•

Guidelines (No. 3)

Finally, some of the activities require people who are sensitive and caring; people who will make good listeners. Who would be the best to include on this basis?

Good listeners	Evidence:
• Safina	• Friends tell her she's a good listener, family get on well together
•	•
•	•

Checkpoint English 2

© HODDER MURRAY

Unit five

Task 4: Choosing the 'Famous Five'

Now it's time to make your final decisions. Working on your own (or as part of the project team), make your selection. A chart has been drawn up to help you with your decisions. It's called a PMI chart (Plus – Minus – Interesting) and all you have to do is put the positive features of each person in the 'P' column, the negative features in the 'M' column and any ideas you have that are not obviously spelt out in the text, in the 'I' column.

> **Skills check: Deduction and inference**
>
> You will be using the skills of deduction during this section because you will be gathering together evidence and coming to your final conclusions. During this section it might make things easier if you talk within a group about what to place in each column. You will then be working collaboratively through speaking and listening to reach decisions.
>
> When you place a comment in the 'I' column (I = Interesting) you will be using inference because you will be making a comment that goes beyond the information you have been given. It's a sort of educated guess. Examples have been given below:

Name	Plus	Minus	Interesting
Ahmed	Outgoing Lots of friends Musical Likes asking questions Plays in a band	Could be awkward to get along with (asks difficult questions)	Wants to be famous – this suggests that he might be a little self-centred
Suzi	Likes people Thoughtful and intelligent Skilful – tapestry Wants the money to go to a worthwhile charity	Doesn't appear to have many friends – could find Little Brother quite difficult	Could be good at the activities because is skilled at tapestry

Unit five

Remember, when you make your final choice, you will need a balance of boys and girls (a gender balance) and a balance of backgrounds (an ethnic balance).

Names	Plus	Minus	Interesting
Tania			
David			
Sarah			
Iaz			
Safina			
Gareth			
Suzi			
Peter			
Avril			
Ahmed			

Checkpoint English 2

Unit five

Task 5: Convince me!

Now that you have made your final choice, you have the more difficult task of preparing yourself to convince others. To do this, you are going to make a presentation to the headteacher and school governors, explaining the project and convincing them that the people you have chosen to take part are the right people.

Firstly, you will need to prepare five 'Speaking Cards' (one on each of the 'Famous Five'), which gather together all of the strong arguments for including them in Little Brother.

Skills check: Making notes	
Your notes will need to be:	
Brief	So that you can use key words to help you to talk in more detail about the candidate to the headteacher and governors
Organised	This will help your talk to make more sense to your audience
Positive	Because you will need to leave out any negative points – remember that your audience needs convincing
Persuasive	Using words that will really persuade your listeners that this school charity event is in good hands

Here's an example of a 'Speaking Card' using the B.O.P.P. idea.

You will notice that the words that could be left out are in brackets. When you are making notes, only include the words that are absolutely necessary.

Long example:

(The) first candidate (we have chosen) is (called) 'X'. (The project) team (were) (really) impressed by (X's) application because:
1. _____
2. _____
3. _____

Summarised example:

First candidate is 'X'. Team impressed by application because:
1. _____
2. _____
3. _____

77

© HODDER MURRAY

Checkpoint English 2

Unit five

Persuasive words

In order to impress your audience and to convince them that you have made the best choices for Little Brother, you will need to use some powerful words that persuade.

As you complete your 'Speaking Cards' try using some of these words as part of your summaries, to give them extra force:

Kind words	Leadership words	Team words	Personality words
Sympathetic	Strong	Involved	Exciting
Caring	Bold	Collaborative	Outgoing
Considerate	Authoritative	Understanding	Adventurous
Thoughtful	Strident	Willing	Interesting
Compliant	Determined	Cooperative	Independent

Use a dictionary to look up their meaning before you include them in your final presentation.

Now you are ready to complete the five 'Speaking Cards' for your list of successful candidates in the Little Brother house. Use the blank version below by copying it for your use.

Candidate _____

Team impressed by application because:

1. _____

2. _____

3. _____

Checkpoint English 2

© HODDER MURRAY

Task 6: Powerful presentations

> **Skills check: Representing information**
> When you 'represent information' you are taking data (in this case what you have to say about Little Brother) and re-arranging it so that it makes sense to someone else.

So, you are given the task of representing all of the Little Brother information so that the headteacher and governors of your school can give the go-ahead for your project.

To do this you need to:

- Decide on the way in which you might present the information, e.g. on an overhead projector or a PowerPoint presentation on the computer.
- Organise a clear account of the project including:
  - What you are doing
  - Why you are doing it
  - Who will be involved
  - How long it will take.

  (Prepare the points above in summary form and put them onto an OHT or in a PowerPoint presentation.)
- Have an image prepared that will help people to picture what will be going on, e.g. in this case, you might want to draw a map of the media studies room that will be turned into the Little Brother house for the day. Be sure to be exact about where the camera will be placed, etc.
- Rehearse the presentation in front of a friend before you deliver it. Be sure to ask for feedback and improve your presentation where necessary.

HELP

Powerful presentations

- Speak clearly
- Make eye contact with your audience
- Explain your ideas
- Use persuasive words
- Use formal English
- Answer questions fully
- Finish by summing up your main points

Unit five

Task 7: Self-evaluation and target-setting

You have come a long way since you agreed to be project manager for the school's charity fund-raiser 'Little Brother'. It's time to review the project and the skills you have learnt.

> **Skills check: Self-evaluation and target-setting**
>
> You have used quite a range of reading, writing, and speaking and listening skills in this unit. Look at the questions below and see if you can work out how well you have done and what you might need to do next in order to improve further.

What skills have I learnt or practised?

Reading:
The next thing I need to do to improve my skimming and scanning is
_____

(Suggestions: Be aware of when these skills are used. Practise them at home when the opportunity arises.)

Writing:
In writing I have _____
_____

In future, I will need to _____
_____

(Suggestions: Remember to use the minimum number of words in a summary. Use powerful persuasive words when I'm trying to convince someone.)

Speaking and Listening:
During the project I have used discussion in the following ways:_____
_____

To improve in the future I will need to _____
_____

(Suggestions: Share my ideas more freely with people. Listen to other people's ideas better. Try to use more formal language when I'm speaking in public.)

UNIT SIX

Shakespeare's Theatre

This unit introduces you to some of the exciting plays written by Shakespeare. As you work through the unit you will build up a factfile on Shakespeare. Copy the factsheet on page 94 and enlarge it if possible. Use the information you find to build up a picture of the life and times of the most famous dramatist of all time.

Shakespeare's life

Factfile

- Shakespeare was born in Stratford-upon-Avon, in England, in 1564.
- His father made gloves.
- Shakespeare married Anne Hathaway in 1582.
- They had two daughters, and a son who died as a boy.
- Shakespeare left his family and went to London.
- He soon joined a theatre, where he started writing plays.
- He wrote about two plays a year when he worked at the Globe Theatre.

Unit six

Shakespeare's times

The next three pages contain information about life in London when Shakespeare was alive and Elizabeth I was the queen of England. Some of the information is in the pictures, and some of it is in the words.

Activity

- Find all the information that tells you about rich people.
  1. Read the words.
  2. See if there are clues in the pictures.
- Write the heading 'Rich People' and make a list of all the facts you find. You don't have to use full sentences. Start like this:

  Rich People

  Lots to buy with money

  Children dressed in the same clothes as adults

  Ate a lot of meat

- Compare your list with other people to check you have got everything. Then in a group write it up in complete sentences. Start like this:

  In Shakespeare's time, rich people were able to buy many luxuries . . .

- Now look for information on one of these topics:

  Clothing

  The streets of London

  Food

  Health

- Share your research with the rest of your class.

Unit six

This painting shows a well-off Elizabethan family. They are saying grace before a meal.

This painting shows poor people eating a meal.

Activity

- Compare the two paintings. Notice the food the people are eating and the clothes they are wearing.

- What do you think life was like in Shakespeare's time:
  a) for rich people?
  b) for poor people?

Four hundred and fifty years ago, when Queen Elizabeth I was alive, London was a very different place from the London of today.

London's muddy, cobbled streets were very noisy. People tried to sell their goods or advertise their trade by shouting things such as, 'Sweet lavender!', 'Any frying pans to mend?' or 'Buy! Buy!'

You could buy custard, coal, apples, sausages, honey (not sugar), mouse traps and rabbits. In fact, you could buy almost anything on the streets of London.

83

Unit six

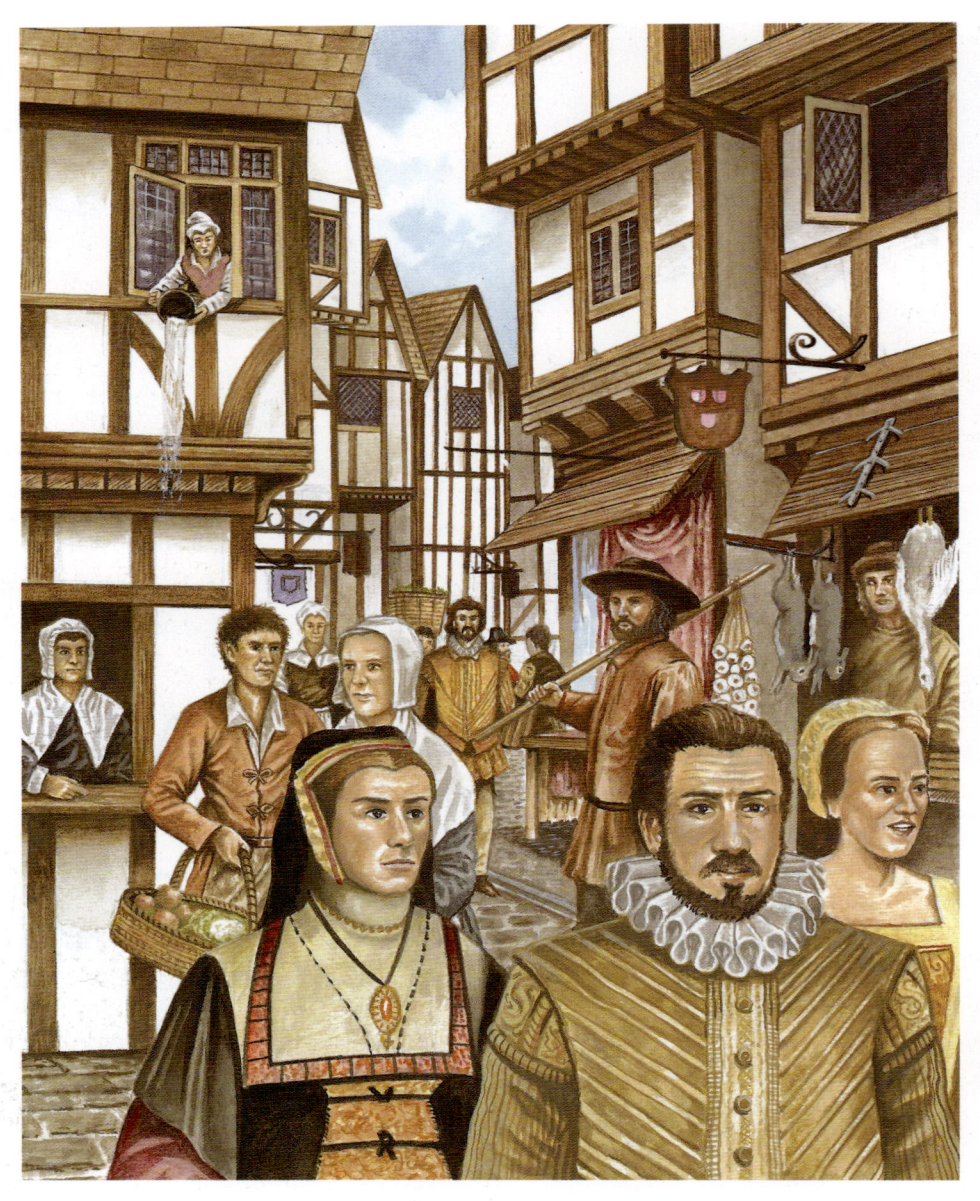

A modern artist's idea of what an Elizabethan street looked like. Each shop had a big window shutter, which folded down to make a counter.

A water carrier

London was a smelly place. There were no drainpipes, just a gutter that ran down the middle of the streets. Everyone threw their rubbish, dirty water and sewage into the gutter.

84

Most ordinary people were smelly too! They rarely washed their hair. Their clothes, which were made of wool, linen and leather, were hardly ever washed. People wore them until they fell apart.

Rich people liked to show others how rich they were. They wore expensive clothes made from silk or velvet that perhaps had fur or feather trims.

Almost every summer there was an outbreak of the plague, which was spread by rats.

Plague deaths in London

Year	No. of people who died
1500	20,000
1563	17,000
1593	10,000
1603	38,000

Unit six

Shakespeare's theatre

John Burbage built the first theatre in 1576. It was round in shape. The Globe Theatre was built in 1599. Shakespeare described it as 'a wooden O'.

The Globe Theatre.
Detail from a map of London, 1616.

People threw apples at the stage if they did not like the play, or if the performance was late.

For one penny you cou[ld] see the play from here with about 1000 others

Unit six

Activity

- Actors had to speak up to be heard in the open air. The characters were larger than life. Can you think of plays that are still like this?

- What difference do you think it made to the actors and their audiences when they performed in theatres rather than the open air?

Musicians played here in the gallery.

Yard

'Hawkers' walked around selling apples, wine, nuts and beer to the audience.

Pickpockets cut the purse strings that hung from people's waists. They were called cutpurse thieves.

These people paid two pence for a seat with a cushion.

People often travelled a long way to get to the theatre. Most of them had to cross London Bridge over the Thames – a long walk if they could not afford a boat.

Unit six

> **Activity**
> - Draw a line down the middle of a piece of paper. On one side, write 'Elizabethan Theatre'. On the other, write 'Modern Theatre'.
> - Write lists, showing the differences between them.
> - Discuss with a partner what it was like to go and see a play at the Globe Theatre. Think about what you might see, hear, touch, smell and taste.
> - On your own, write a short description of going to the theatre yourself in Shakespeare's day.

The stage

This diagram shows what it was like on the stage and behind the scenes.

1. Machinery for lowering actors to the stage
2. Storage
3. The 'Heavens'
4. Pulley system
5. Balcony
6. Props room
7. Dressing room and wardrobe
8. Back stage (the tiring house)
9. Props
10. Stage trap door
11. The 'Hell'

Unit six

Activity

Working with a partner, match the numbers on the diagram to the descriptions below. Write your answers like this: 1 A

A	Lifting gear for actors	G	The 'Heavens'
B	Backstage	H	The balcony
C	Storage space	I	Props room
D	The 'Hell'	J	Pulley system
E	Stage trap door	K	Dressing room and wardrobe
F	Props		

Factfile

- Women were not allowed to act.
- Costumes were very expensive. Players were fined if they left the theatre in their costumes.
- There were very few props.
- There was one door on each side of the stage.
- There was no scenery.
- Sometimes rich people sat in the gallery with the musicians to watch the play and show off their finery! (A bit like sitting in a royal box in a modern theatre.)

Activity

Work out the answers to these questions. Write your answers down in full sentences.

1. If women were not allowed to act, who played the female characters?
2. If there was no scenery, how did the audience know where the play was set, what time of day it was, or what the weather was like?
3. What problems can you see with having no roof?
4. How could the actors use:
   - the balcony
   - the trap door
   - the lifting gear?

Unit six

Shakespeare's language

Shakespeare's language can be quite difficult to read. This is partly because it is old. People expressed themselves differently in the past. Shakespeare puts together unusual and descriptive words so each line is packed with meaning. But sometimes, he uses language as we do today. You can have some good fun with it! Read on to see how.

Insults

On the next page is a list of insults from Shakespeare's plays.

Activity

- Practise reading the insults.
- Choose three of your favourite insults. Remember them.
- As a class, stand in a circle and insult the person opposite you. (It's OK – it's Shakespeare!)
- Experiment with the way you say them:
    - shout
    - whisper
    - speak through gritted teeth
    - scream
    - be nasty
    - be snooty

★ Glossary

carrion = *dead animal flesh*

hag-seed = *someone whose mother is a witch*

prodigal = *someone who has behaved very badly*

lean-witted = *not very clever*

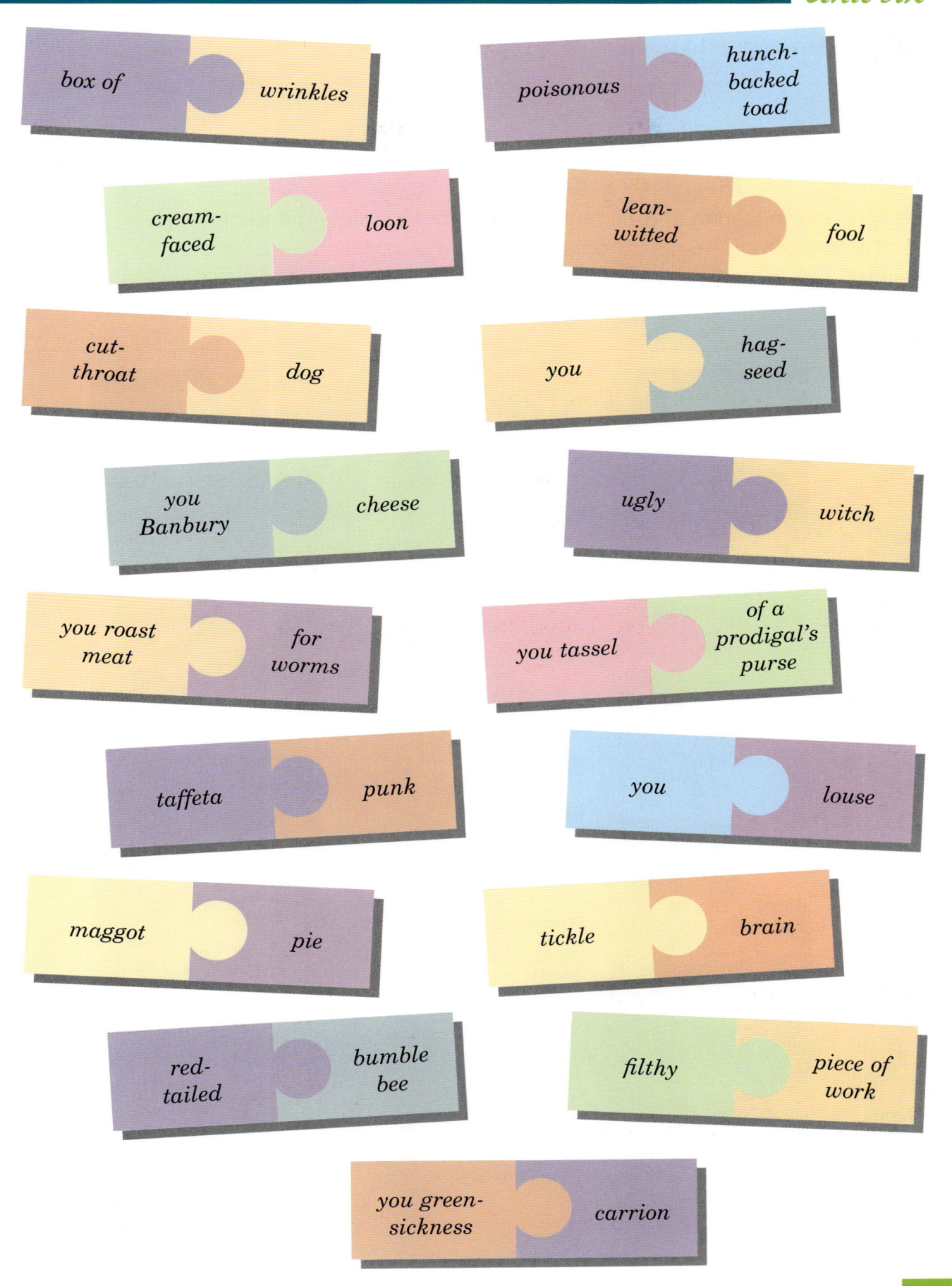

Unit six

- box of / wrinkles
- poisonous / hunch-backed toad
- cream-faced / loon
- lean-witted / fool
- cut-throat / dog
- you / hag-seed
- you Banbury / cheese
- ugly / witch
- you roast meat / for worms
- you tassel / of a prodigal's purse
- taffeta / punk
- you / louse
- maggot / pie
- tickle / brain
- red-tailed / bumble bee
- filthy / piece of work
- you green-sickness / carrion

Unit six

You are now going to make a game called 'insults'.

Activity

Using a copy of the page of insults (page 91):

- Cut out the insult jigsaw pieces
- Mix up the insults and piece them together to make different ones. Try to think of the most horrible insults you can
- Using Shakespeare's style, try making up some of your own insults (without using foul language!)

Read this scene from Shakespeare's play *Macbeth*. The witches chant as they mix a magic potion in the cauldron:

1st Witch	Round about the cauldron go;
	In the poisoned entrails throw...
ALL	Double, double, toil and trouble;
	Fire burn, and cauldron bubble.
2nd Witch	Fillet of a fenny snake,
	In the cauldron boil and bake;
	Eye of newt, and toe of frog,
	Wool of bat, and tongue of dog,
	Adder's fork and blind-worm's sting,
	Lizard's leg and howlet's wing,
	For a charm of powerful trouble,
	Like a hell-broth boil and bubble.
ALL	Double, double, toil and trouble;
	Fire burn, and cauldron bubble.
3rd Witch	Scale of dragon, tooth of wolf,
	Witches' mummy, maw and gulf
	Of the ravined salt-sea shark,
	Root of hemlock digged i' the dark...
ALL	Double, double, toil and trouble;
	Fire burn, and cauldron bubble.

(*Macbeth*, Act 4, Scene 1)

Activity

- What do the witches put in the cauldron? Make a list using modern words.
- In groups of three, work out some ideas for ingredients for your own magic potion. Think about things you can see, hear, smell, touch and taste.
- Write your own version of the witches' chant. Try to use the same layout and style as Shakespeare.
- Act out your version for the class. Try to remember your lines, rather than reading them.

WILLIAM SHAKESPEARE

Date born:

Place of birth:

Father's job:

Wife's name:

Occupation:

Place of work:

Portrait

The Globe Theatre

Shakespeare's Language

Life in London

Places to Visit

UNIT SEVEN

Marvel or Monster? Right or Wrong?

Read the following information.

WHAT IS GENETIC ENGINEERING?

Engineering is another word for making things. *Genetic engineering* is making things with *genetics*, or *genes*.

AND WHAT ARE GENES?

Genes are found in all living things, or *organisms*. They carry the code for life. If you like, genes are a recipe for making people – or anything else that lives, i.e. plant or animal.

Genetic engineering, then, is about scientists altering the recipe for life. They do this using the very latest technology. They can snip a gene from one organism and splice it into another. This might help the organism to grow faster, or fight disease, or live longer.

WHY ARE PEOPLE WORRIED ABOUT GENETIC ENGINEERING?

Grow faster? Fight disease? Live longer? This all sounds fantastic. However, there are lots of worries about genetic engineering. It is a new science and no one is sure what the long-term effects of altering recipes for life might be.

This cartoon is from the oneworld website, Tiki the Penguin's guide to genetic engineering – www.oneworld.net/penguin/genetics/home.html

You might like to draw your own cartoon to represent what genetic engineering is – for example, a scientist trying to make a new creature out of a fish and a carrot!

Activity

You may not be familiar with all the ideas and words on this page. Read it again carefully and write down three questions you would like to ask your teacher about genetic engineering. Compare questions with a partner and select your best three.

Unit seven

Frankenfears

This is not a new topic. People have long been scared of what science can do.

An early example is the story of *Frankenstein*, written by Mary Shelley in 1818. Read this passage, which describes the thoughts of Dr Frankenstein as his monster comes to life. The monster was made by fitting together the different body parts of dead people – what could be called *human engineering*.

> It was on a dreary night of November that I beheld the accomplishment of my toils. With an anxiety that almost amounted to agony, I collected the instruments of life around me, that I might infuse a spark of being into the lifeless thing that lay at my feet. It was already one in the morning; the rain pattered dismally against the panes, and my candle was nearly burnt out, when, by the glimmer of the half-extinguished light, I saw the dull yellow eye of the creature open; it breathed hard, and a convulsive motion agitated its limbs.
>
> How can I describe my emotions at this catastrophe, or how delineate the wretch whom with such infinite pains and care I had endeavoured to form? His limbs were in proportion, and I had selected his features as beautiful. Beautiful! Great God! His yellow skin scarcely covered the work of muscles and arteries beneath; his hair was of a lustrous black, and flowing; his teeth of pearly whiteness; but these luxuriances only formed a more horrid contrast with his watery eyes, that seemed almost of the same colour as the dun-white sockets in which they were set, his shrivelled complexion and straight black lips.
>
> . . . I had worked hard for nearly two years, for the sole purpose of infusing life into an inanimate body. For this I had deprived myself of rest and health . . . but now that I had finished, the beauty of the dream vanished, and breathless horror and disgust filled my heart.

Activity

Discuss with a partner:

1. What are Dr Frankenstein's feelings as the monster comes to life?
2. Pick out five phrases that show a mood of fear and menace in this passage. Try to explain how they create this mood. This one is done for you: 'the dull yellow eye of the creature…' This shows that the 'creature' is not like a human – 'dull yellow' sounds more like an animal.

Unit seven

Facts stranger than fiction

Science and fiction are coming closer and closer together. Everything below has already happened. Discuss in pairs, and then fill in a photocopy of the chart to help form your opinion about genetic engineering.

WHAT SCIENCE HAS DONE:	WHY MIGHT THIS BE USEFUL?	DO I THINK IT IS WRONG OR RIGHT?	WHY SHOULD THIS CONTINUE / STOP?
This is Dolly the sheep. She was the world's first clone. This means she is an exact copy of another sheep.			
This fish is a genetically modified carp. It has been treated with human growth hormone genes to make it bigger.			
Scientists can genetically modify crops, such as corn, so that they grow much bigger than other crops.			
Scientists can genetically modify the organs in pigs (such as the heart) so that they can be transplanted into humans.			

© HODDER MURRAY

Checkpoint English 2

Unit seven

A moral maze

Imagine you are a politician in a 'Future Government'. Discuss the cards below in small groups, and agree on your answer to the final question. Select one card on which to report back to the class. Make notes, using the speaking frame on the page opposite to help. Remember to use your notes as prompts for speaking – don't just read them out.

Designer babies

Cloning of human beings is now possible. This means that exact copies of people can be made. So if you want a son or a daughter to look exactly like you, then you can have one made to order. The Government has been asked to pass a law allowing the cloning of humans. Should such a law be passed?

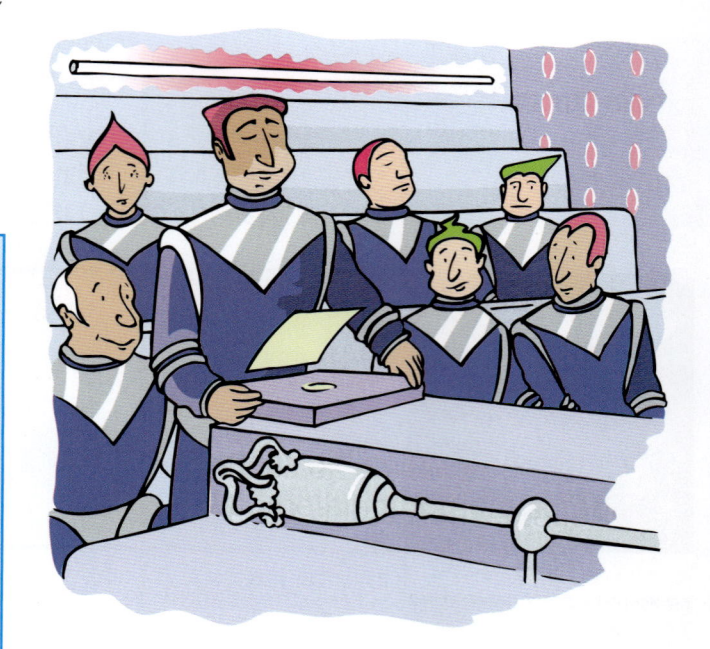

Living for 200 years

The genes that make people grow old have been found by scientists. They can engineer these genes so that people can live much longer than at present. Most people, the scientists say, will be able to live to be 200 years old. The Government has been asked to pass a law to allow this science to be used. Should such a law be passed?

Spinning silk from goats' milk

Scientists can splice the gene from a silk worm into the gene that makes goats' milk. There is no harm to the goat, but the genetically engineered milk can be used to spin silk cheaply and quickly. The Government has been asked to pass a law to allow this science to be used. Should such a law be passed?

A pig's heart for people

Scientists can grow organs (like the heart, kidneys, liver) in pigs that can easily be transplanted into humans. The pigs, however, often suffer pain and, obviously, are killed when a human needs one of its organs. The Government has been asked to pass a law to allow this science to be used. Should such a law be passed?

Unit seven

A balanced argument

Present *your* ideas using a *balanced argument*. You will probably not put a great deal of *emphasis* on your words until the end, when you put forward your own ideas.

> Our topic for discussion has been . . .
>
> The positive aspects of this scientific advance are as follows . . .
>
> However, there are also possible negative aspects. These are . . .
>
> Overall, it is our belief that a law should/should not be passed to allow this science to be used. We believe this for the following reasons . . .

HELP

An effective speech

- Is well-organised so that the points come across clearly
- Uses repetition and emphasis to make key points
- Uses evidence and real-life examples
- Captures the attention of the listeners with a clear voice and eye-contact.

Extension task

Rewrite your argument so that it is no longer balanced. Instead, argue very strongly for one side or the other, without looking at both the positive and negative effects carefully.

- What tone will you use to deliver this speech?
- To which words will you give extra emphasis?

Unit seven

Changing humans

Human genetic engineering could have a massive impact on human life in years to come. Read about some of the possibilities below. As you read, try to decide what your own opinions are on the subject. Do you agree, disagree or are you unable to make up your mind? Why?

**Professor Heal:
helping to stop hereditary diseases**

My interest in human genetic engineering is in stopping families passing on disabilities from one generation to the next. If you are born with a disability, it is sometimes because it has come from your parents' genes. I am working on technology that will change those genes, so there is no chance of a disease being passed on. This will lead to more healthy people being born. It will make parents and children feel happier. Also, it will save the National Health Service millions of pounds in caring for people with disabilities.

**Professor Long:
helping people to live longer**

My interest in human genetic engineering is in helping people live longer. What can be wrong with that? Everyone wants to live longer, so long as they are healthy. It is not possible at the moment, but it could be in the near future. Scientists are developing ways of growing human organs and cells outside the body, so that they can be stored and used to replace old ones. Also, they have found the gene that makes the body repair itself. If they can change this, they can make the body repair itself for much longer periods of time.

Professor Copy: cloning humans

My interest in human genetic engineering is in helping people make perfect copies (clones) of themselves. This cannot be done at the moment, but it might happen in the near future. I would not make it available to everyone. Instead, I would allow clones of people who have achieved great things in life. This could be through their intelligence or through their physical skill and strength. In this way the human race will improve.

Making notes

Make notes on the views and ideas of each professor under the following headings:

- A summary of their ideas
- What I like about their ideas
- What I do not like about their ideas

HELP

- Use bullets or numbers to make a list (just like this!)
- Don't copy from the text. Decide what is the main point or idea and note it down
- No need to use full sentences (just like this!)

Report on human genetics

Politicians are worried about how quickly the science of human genetic engineering is developing. They want a carefully written report that gives the *facts* about what is going on. They also want a strong opinion about which work is safe and which could be dangerous.

They have asked you to write a report. The report must do two things:

1. Explain what different scientists are doing.
2. Argue what you think is safe and what you think is dangerous.

Use your notes from the previous frame and the writing frame below to write your report. Don't write on the frame. Have it alongside you as you draft your report.

Report on developments in human genetic engineering

<u>The Scientific Process</u>

Scientists are exploring three main areas of human genetic engineering. These are:

1. _____

2. _____

3. _____

The first involves _____

The second involves _____

The third involves _____

<u>What is safe and what is dangerous?</u>

In my opinion research into _____

should/should not continue.

It benefits/is dangerous for the human race

Firstly because _____

Secondly _____

Finally _____

Repeat this paragraph for each of the three areas of human genetic engineering.

Unit seven

GM crops: do you know what you eat?

Genetically modified crops

Scientists have been changing the genes in crops, such as corn, to make them grow bigger and quicker. Also, the crops can be changed to fight disease more easily. These crops are called *Genetically Modified*, or *GM*, crops. There are lots of arguments about the safety of GM crops. You will look at these arguments on the next few pages.

Firstly, read the leaflet from a company called MonsterAntCo. They want to test GM crops in your local area. They have written a leaflet to local people trying to persuade them to let the crops be tested.

Dear Local People,

GM crops have the power to change the world. FOREVER.

GM crops have the power to wipe out crop disease. FOREVER.

GM crops have the power to eliminate world hunger. FOREVER.

These are big claims. Correction. These are **MASSIVE** claims. But let's look at the facts to see how they could come true.

GM crops have been genetically engineered in some way. This means that their genetic code has been altered to make them grow **STRONGER, FASTER AND HEALTHIER.**

This means that more food can be grown in a shorter period of time. And it is disease-free. So there is more food to feed the whole world. And the world changes for the better.

You might have heard some other things about GM crops. We admit we do not yet know all the facts. That is why it is important to run tests. We want to grow some test crops in your area. Please let us do this. You could be helping to change the world. **FOREVER**.

Activity

In a group, discuss together:

1. What does the company want people in the community to do?
2. Pick out three ways the leaflet tries to *persuade* you. You might comment on: words and phrases; layout; use of repeated words or phrases; other features you notice.

A sour taste: the opposing argument

The leaflet from MonsterAntCo ignores a lot of concerns that many people have about GM crops. Some of these concerns are listed below.

MonsterAntCo failed to mention that:
- GM crops might harm your health
- GM crops might be so powerful that other natural crops would be wiped out
- GM crops might harm or even kill local wildlife
- The pollen from GM crops tests can spread many miles. Therefore, there is no way of controlling where the crops are grown
- There should be enough food to feed the whole world already
- Big companies like MonsterAntCo make farmers buy their GM seeds. This makes small farmers poorer and big companies richer.

Select what you think are the three most important concerns and use them in a postcard to be sent to MonsterAntCo as part of a campaign to stop GM crops being grown.

Dear Chief Executive,

You must halt tests of GM crops until much more is known about them.
Firstly ...
Also ...
Finally ...

Yours sincerely,

Chief Executive,
MonsterAntCo,
Corporate Drive,
Goldtown

Unit seven

The great crop debate

MonsterAntCo is still trying to test Genetically Modified crops in your local area. A decision has not yet been taken.

You are going to take part in a debate in which all sides of the argument are heard.

Read the points below, made by each of the four main speakers. Share out the roles in your group of four.

Local Farmer: AGAINST
- Already grows plenty of food
- Does not want his other crops spoiled by GM crops
- Will have to buy GM seeds in the future. At the moment can use his own seeds that are free
- GM crops, in the long run, will mean small farms getting taken over by big farms

MonsterAntCo Manager: FOR
- GM crops will lead to more food for everyone
- GM crops are safe
- The tests are carefully controlled
- GM crops will lead to more food and so more profits for farmers
- Farmers do not have to buy GM seeds if they do not want to

Eco-warrior: AGAINST
- GM crops risk destroying nature
- GM crops might be unsafe to eat
- GM crops mean small farmers go out of business
- GM crops help companies like MonsterAntCo make massive profits
- There should already be enough food for everyone

Local Politician: FOR
- The tests need to take place somewhere
- GM crops could help feed the whole world
- Companies like MonsterAntCo will bring business to the area
- Parliament will make sure the tests are controlled
- People will still be able to choose what they eat

Powerful speech

Use this sequence to write a powerful speech as your character.

Plan in note form what you want to say and the key evidence you will use to back up your argument.

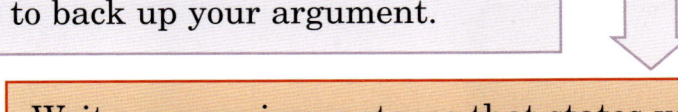

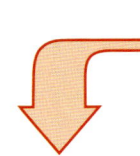

Write an opening sentence that states your opinion. **Use one of the following strong modal verbs**: *must, should, could, can, might, may, ought to.*

Continue your first paragraph, explaining why you feel so strongly and use some evidence to back up what you say.

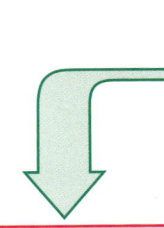

Write a strong opening (topic) sentence for a second paragraph. Use repetition: in speeches, it is a good idea to repeat a word or a phrase for emphasis, e.g. <u>No to</u> strange science, <u>no to</u> MonsterAntCo, <u>no to</u> GM crops!

Write up one of your points using a repeated word or phrase.

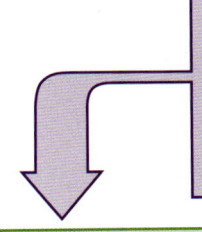

Conclude your speech in a final paragraph. Say **why** you believe what you do, and use another good example to prove your point. Try to finish on a strong note, e.g. 'So I urge you all to support me and to do everything you can to . . .'

Finally: read through what you have written. It is important to order your points carefully and in the correct order. If you haven't already done so, fit in some **connectives** to link up your ideas. Use some or all of these connectives to order your speech: *first, next, then, moreover, additionally, also, finally.*

Unit seven

Actions speak louder than words

It is now time to deliver your speech.

Try not to read from the script. Instead make notes to look at from time to time.

Here are some good ideas about delivery.

Stand straight, tall and in one place.

Cast your glance over the whole audience as you speak.

Make gestures to emphasise key points, e.g. punch air or bang fist down for a strong idea.

Hold your hands out in front of you.

UNIT EIGHT

Horror

Beginnings

Look at these opening scenes from an episode of *The X Files* – a TV series exploring the paranormal and other mysterious happenings.

Unit eight

Activity

- Imagine that you are Randall. Note down all the mysteries you do not understand. Set your work out like this:

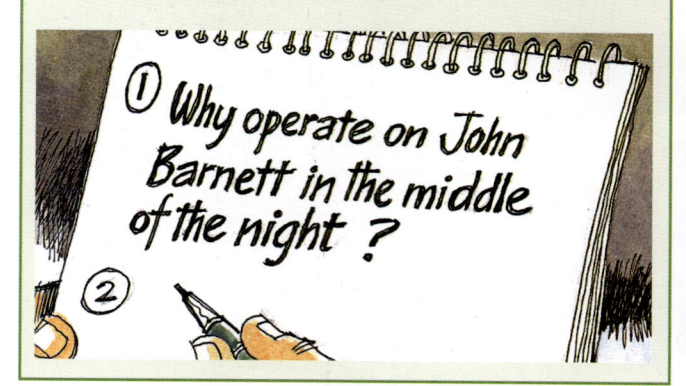

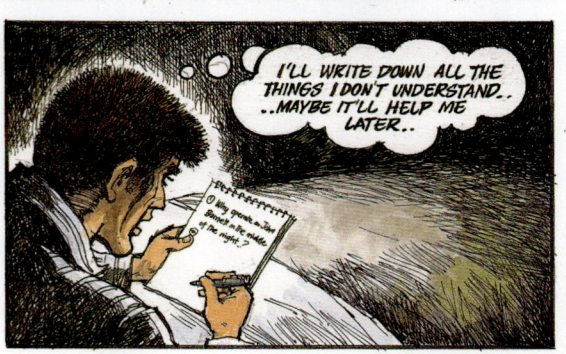

Activity

Discuss the following questions in groups:

- Why do film makers like to start a horror film with a mystery?
- How long do you have to wait for the answers to the mysteries – until the middle of the story, or the end?
- Why do you think you are made to wait for mysteries to be solved?
- Can you think of other horror films or books that have beginnings as mysterious as this?

Unit eight

A place of horror

Activity

Look at these settings for horror stories and read the extract from *Dracula*, below.
- In what ways are the settings similar?
- How are they different?

A vast ruined castle, from whose tall black windows came no ray of light, and whose broken battlements showed a jagged line against the moonlit sky…

From *Dracula* by Bram Stoker

Activity

List ten words you could use to describe a setting for a horror story, e.g. dank.

109

Unit eight

Horror train

Now it's your chance to write a mystery opening to a horror story called 'Horror Train'.

Activity

Look at the cartoon. Continue the story. Keep the mystery going!

- Think about what the kids feel as the train comes closer.
- Why does it get colder as the train approaches?
- What happens when the train stops?
- Are there any passengers? If so, what do they look like?
- Do the kids get on the train?
- You might use these starters to help you with the first few sentences, or you can make up your own.

As the train came closer, the kids felt…

As the train neared the platform, they could see…

Something was strange about the passengers. They all looked…

There was a smell of…

The worst thing of all was the…

As the doors opened…

Unit eight

Create your own monster

When a crime has been committed the police make a 'photofit' of the criminal. They do this by fitting together photos of eyes, mouth and other features.

Activity
- Create your own photofit monster by fitting together features from the monsters on these pages.
- Invent a name for your monster.

Fachan was an Irish monster with one leg and one eye. Its only hand stuck out of its chest. It chased travellers and jumped on them from behind.

A **banshee** was a wailing woman with fiery red eyes, webbed feet and long streaming hair. She had one nostril and a front tooth that stuck out. A banshee would sit crying on the banks of a river, washing the clothes of a person who was about to die.

Unit eight

Jenny Greenteeth was an evil creature who lived underwater. She drowned anyone who went near the green scum on the surface of the water. This green scum was the only clue to where she was. It was all that anyone ever saw…

A **basilisk** was a serpent. It was so deadly that if a man put a spear through its body, the poison would spread up the spear and kill the man and his horse. A basilisk could kill by its look or its breath. But it could be killed by its own reflection, or by the crowing of a cockerel.

Activity

- Make up a monster of your own. Draw your monster.
- Underneath your drawing write a description of the monster:
    1. Describe what your monster can do to people.
    2. Explain how it can be killed.

Unit eight

Hanging on

Horror stories must be exciting, to make us want to read on. Writers of horror stories often use cliffhanger endings to build up excitement at the end of a chapter. Look at how the author builds up the tension in the extract below.

Lost in the Woods

Susan Cooper has just moved to a new house, deep in the woods. She gets up early to explore without her older brother Mickey, but gets lost…

I returned to the path again. But with my first step, I heard leaves rustling behind me. I didn't turn round. I quickened my pace.

And I heard it again.

Twigs snapping. Leaves rustling.

My throat suddenly felt dry. Don't panic. Don't panic. 'Who – who's there?' I croaked.

No answer.

I turned back.

Whoa! Which way had I been walking? My head began to spin. I suddenly felt dizzy.

Too dizzy to remember where I had been. *Snap. Snap. Crack. Crunch.*

'Who is there?' I called out again. My voice didn't sound all that steady for Super Cooper.

'Mickey, is that you? This isn't funny! Mickey?'

Then I felt something horrible scrape my cheek. Something cold. And sharp.

I couldn't help it. I started to scream.

From *The Barking Ghost* by R. L. Stine

Activity

- What do you think is the 'something horrible' that is scraping Susan's cheek? What is going on?

- Discuss what you think is going to happen in the next chapter.

- Now read what actually did happen in the next chapter.

Unit eight

A leaf. A dumb leaf.

Come on Cooper! Get a grip!

Did you get it right? Even if you didn't, you kept on reading – and that is what the writer wanted you to do.

Cliffhanger endings make us want to read on – just like a chapter that ends with the hero hanging from a cliff!

Dead Man's Bay

Now try writing a cliffhanger of your own, starting with the story below.

Jenny has gone on holiday to Dead Man's Bay. Her parents have forbidden her to swim in the bay because sharks have been seen there in the past. But Jenny thinks her parents are making a fuss as usual. She gets up early and goes to Dead Man's Bay for a secret swim…

The story begins like this:

Dead Man's Bay was exactly as Jenny had hoped. A perfect stretch of empty yellow beach. A beautiful, blue sea.

And not a shark fin in sight.

Wait until she got back and told her parents she had been swimming in Dead Man's Bay, and nothing had happened! Quickly, she stripped to her swimming costume. Then she sprinted towards the sparkling white surf and dived in.

At first, it was…

Activity

- First finish the chapter. Take the story up to a really frightening point – and stop.
- Write the first few lines of the **next** chapter. Here you can show that Jenny wasn't really in danger after all.
- Swap first chapter cliffhangers with a partner. Do **not** pass over your next chapter.
- Try to guess each other's cliffhanger.
- Now swap second chapters and see if you were right.

115

Unit eight

Building up tension

Look at these two versions of a scene:

Version A

When Michael reached David's house it was dark. He went in and looked around for a bit. He found David dead in the bath. David had been killed by an escaped murderer, who was still hiding in the loft.

Version B

When Michael arrived at his friend's house it was pitch black. To his surprise the front door was ajar. He pushed gently and the door swung inwards.

'David…?' he called softly.

There was no answer.

There was a noise from the sitting room. Michael peered in, but there was only the television.

'Here is the six o'clock news,' said the announcer. 'A dangerous murderer has escaped from a local prison –'

Michael switched it off. Who cared about boring old news?

Suddenly he felt something cold on his nose. He put up his hand and it came away wet. Quickly he went to the stairs, and climbed to the landing. The sound of running water came from the bathroom.

'David, why on earth are you…?'

But his words froze on his lips at the sight of a claw-like hand gripping the edge of the bath.

And blood running down the side…

'David!' he cried.

Through a crack in the ceiling a cruel eye watched Michael rush to his friend.

Activity

- Which version builds up the tension best?
- How is the tension built up?
- Which version do you prefer?
- What do you like reading about in that version?

Unit eight

Activity

Now continue the story as Michael tries to escape from the house.

- Start when Michael looks up and sees the murderer's eye through a hole in the bathroom ceiling.
- Use any of the ideas suggested above to build up tension, as Michael struggles to escape.
- You can use these starters to help you write the first few sentences, or you can make up your own.

Suddenly Michael had a terrible feeling that he was being…

It was an eye…

At that moment he remembered the news on the television. Immediately he knew…

He did not want to leave his friend David in the bath, but…

- The ending is up to you. It could be a cliffhanger ending.

Unit eight

Dracula lives!

Dracula is the most famous monster. Dracula has a human body but can change into a bat. He has long teeth that he sinks into the necks of his victims to drink their blood. But on the surface he is still a normal man, except for one or two details . . .

It was a strong face, with peculiar arched nostrils and high domed forehead. His eyebrows were massive. The mouth was fixed and rather cruel looking, with sharp white teeth, which hung over his lip. For the rest, his ears were pale and at the tops extremely pointed, the chin was broad and strong, the cheeks firm though thin.

Strange to say, there were hairs in the centre of his palms. The nails were long and fine, and cut to a sharp point. As the Count leaned over me and his hands touched me, I could not repress a shudder. It may have been that his breath was rank, but a horrible feeling of sickness came over me. I heard from down below in the valley, the howling of many wolves. The Count's eyes gleamed and he said: 'Listen to them – the children of the night. What music they make!'

From *Dracula* by Bram Stoker

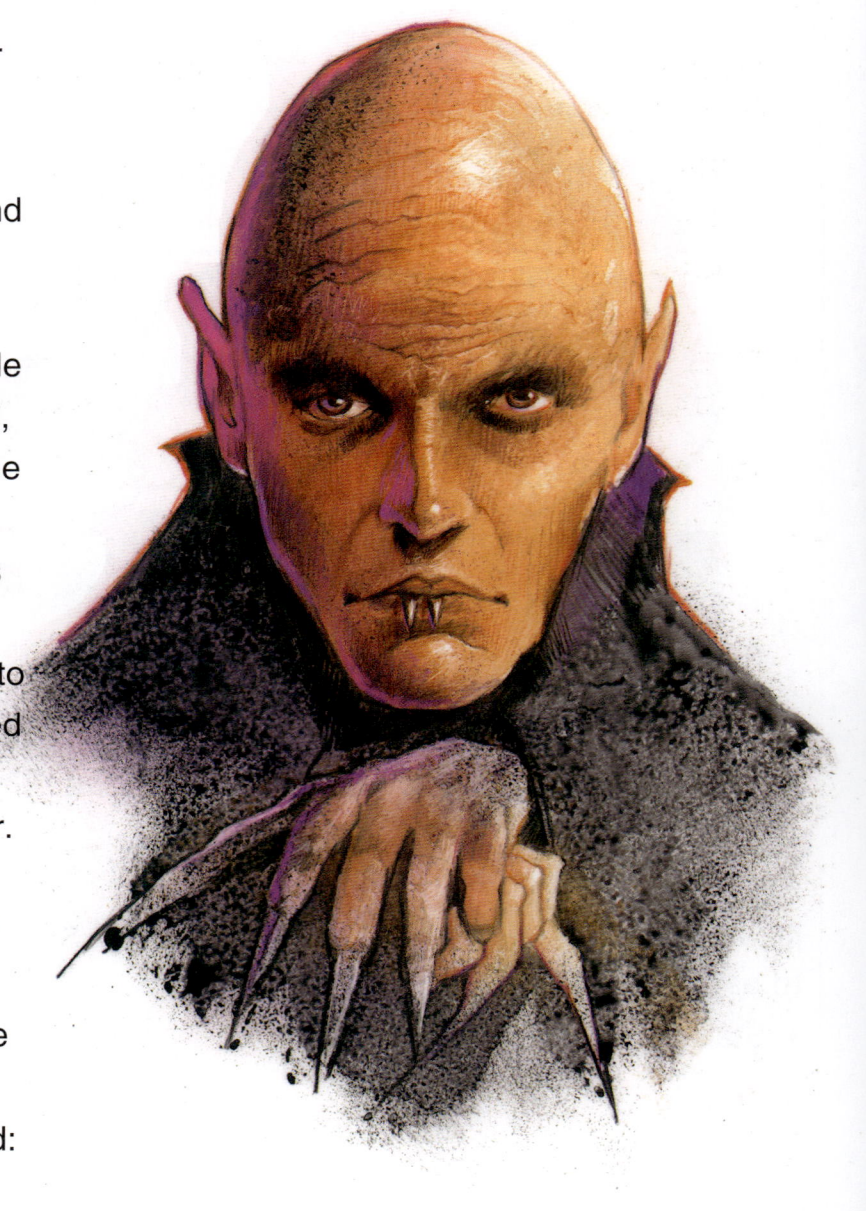

Activity

1. Work out how the writer warns the reader about the Count.

    - Find five clues in the passage that warn you that the Count is a vampire.
    - Find two words or phrases that hint that he is dangerous.
    - Find three clues that suggest he is not part of the normal world.

2. Most of the sentences are descriptive. What do the rest do? Find examples of:

    - The narrator's private thoughts and feelings
    - Action – something happens
    - Speech – someone speaks.

3. Write half a page describing a school visitor you have been asked to take to the Science lab. You can't help noticing something odd.

    You must include:

    - Clues to warn the reader
    - A glimpse into your own feelings
    - An action that happens as you walk over
    - The visitor speaking.

4. Share your description with three other people and decide what worked well.

Unit eight

Horrible horror

> But my feelings changed to revulsion and terror when I saw the whole man slowly emerge from the window and begin to crawl down the castle wall over the dreadful abyss, *face down*, with his cloak spreading out around him like great wings. At first I could not believe my eyes. I thought it was some trick of the moonlight, some weird effect of shadow; but I kept looking, and it could be no delusion. I saw the fingers and toes grasp the corners of the stones, worn clear of the mortar by the stress of years, and thus using every projection and inequality move downwards with considerable speed, just as a lizard moves along a wall.
>
> From *Dracula* by Bram Stoker

- Find three ways the writer describes the woman's feelings.
- Find three ways the writer makes Dracula look like a creature.

Notice that nothing actually happens in this extract. The most powerful actions are written as description.

Unit eight

Activity

- Write the story of a fight between you and one of the monsters in the pictures on pages 112–113. Describe your struggle to survive.
- Follow these steps. You can use the sentence starters shown, or you can make up your own. Try to use at least **two** more sentences of your own each time.

  1. You confront the monster:

     It was the ugliest sight I had ever seen . . .

  2. Describe the monster's reaction to you:

     It gave a snarl of hate . . .

  3. Describe your feelings:

     I could barely breathe, I was so frightened . . .

  4. The monster attacks first:

     It gave a sudden terrible lunge . . .

  5. Describe its strength:

     Its long fingers cut into my flesh and . . .

  6. Describe how you fight back:

     I summoned all my strength to twist from its grip . . .

  7. Describe how it fights back:

     Enraged, the monster . . .

  8. Describe how you finally get the better of it:

     At that moment, I . . .

HELP

Writing action

The easiest thing about action is deciding what happens. The tricky bit is making the reader feel involved and excited.
  It helps if you:

- spend a third of your words on the action
- spend a third of your words on description
- spend a third of your words on thoughts and feelings
- choose verbs that are rich and strong, e.g. 'grasped' rather than 'held', 'seized' rather than 'got', 'slumped' rather than 'fell'.

Unit eight

The beast must die

Horror films and books usually end with the death of the monster. At the end of *Dracula*, the Count has been tracked back to his castle. He thinks he is safe, because night is about to fall:

The sun was almost down on the mountain top, and the shadows of the whole group fell long upon the snow. I saw the Count lying within the box upon the earth. He was deathly pale, just like a waxen image, and the red eyes glared with the horrible look I knew too well.

As I looked, the eyes saw the sinking sun, and the look of hate in them turned to triumph.

But, on the instant, came the sweep and flash of Jonathan's great knife. I shrieked as I saw it shear through the throat; whilst at the same time Mr Morris's bowie knife plunged into the heart.

It was like a miracle; but before our eyes, and almost in the drawing of a breath, the whole body crumbled into dust and passed from our sight.

I shall be glad as long as I live that even in that moment of death there was in that face a look of peace, such as I never could have imagined.

From *Dracula* by Bram Stoker

Activity

In this original version, Dracula's head is cut off.

- Decide on a different death for Dracula. Four ideas are given here. You can use one of these, or perhaps you know another way of killing vampires.

Dracula is terrified of the sign of the cross. You chase him towards a windmill. Dracula turns to attack you. But he has not noticed the shape that the sails of the windmill make. The shape is a cross…

Vampires cannot survive in running water. You are chasing Dracula, but he tries to escape by crossing a river. The water is rough and you start to swim after the boat…

Dracula cannot survive in daylight. Instead he sleeps in a coffin during the day. But you manage to break through into the chamber where the coffin lies. You pull back the heavy curtains, letting in the light. Then you go towards the coffin…

Dracula can be killed with a stake through the heart. You corner Dracula in his castle. Dracula bares his teeth. You have no weapon. Then you notice a display of knives on the wall…

Activity

- Now write your own 'Death of Dracula'.

Unit eight

From picture to page

Go back to page 107 and read the first six cartoon boxes that start the story. Work in a group to convert them into the opening of a written story.

You have:

- The events in order
- The speech

You need to add:

- A narrator to tell the story
- Description (because in a written story there are no pictures)
- Some spooky details to get the mood right
- An insight into Randall's thoughts

HELP

Concentrate on:

- Creating an atmosphere
- Raising questions in the reader's mind
- Building up tension.

Horror is not so much about events, but more about fear of events.

From page to picture

Go back to 'Lost in the Woods' on page 114 and plan how you could convert it into six cartoon or storyboard boxes. You don't have to draw it – matchstick men will do.

- What can you keep?
- What must you lose?

HELP

Storyboards

You can use:

- Pictures
- Speech bubbles
- Thought bubbles
- Essential captions at the top of the picture
- Signs in the picture.

Can you think of other ways of communicating in cartoons? For example, shock bubbles, split screens, symbols such as question marks.

Usage Activities

The Usage section consists of exercises to help those pupils who may need to focus more attention on sentence structure and use of punctuation. Teachers may find it helpful to use the unpunctuated extracts, which are generally linked to the units through subject content, as a basis for whole-class or group-led discussions on the effect punctuation has on meaning and comprehension.

Usage – Unit One

Conditionals

There are times when you need to express ideas that you cannot be sure about. You may need to write about the possibility or probability of something happening or the fact that something could happen only in certain circumstances.

> **HELP**
>
> These words and phrases will help when you are writing about something you are not completely certain about.
>
> Possibility – perhaps, maybe, could, might, may
>
> Probability – it is likely that, probably, in all likelihood, expect, should, seems as though
>
> Only in certain circumstances – if only, if…, then, on condition that, when…, then, but only if

Usage activities

Pick out the seven conditional clauses from the text below. The first one has been done for you.

> That's a lovely painting, Natalie. <u>When it's done,</u> we can put it on the wall. No, don't do that, or I might take the brush away. Put it down, Natalie. Natalie, put the brush down or else I'll be cross. Yes, I know George likes blue, but not on his back. Put it down! George's Mummy will be very cross if she sees him in that state. Now, don't cry, George. Thank you, Ali, that's very thoughtful of you. Let's get some water and see if we can wash it off. That's better. If you behave, we'll have a story.

Punctuation

Unit One has many speaking and listening activities. When you are writing direct speech remember that you need to use speech marks and that the speaker tag can be in different parts of the sentence. Revise your use of speech marks on the following conversation. Copy it out, adding speech marks and any other punctuation that may be missing. Also underline the speech tags.

> The two friends sat down to drink from their cans and began to think of the end of term
>   What are you going to do in the holidays asked Clare Do you have any plans
>   I am going to stay with my cousins for a week replied Julie I go every year What about you
>   We hire a caravan and drive to the coast We stay at the same place every year It's great actually but I get bored in the car
>   Julie agreed I think the best bit about holidays is being at home and having time to do things I enjoy that as much as being away
>   I can't wait said Clare

HELP

Examples

'Do you want to come for a swim?' <u>Tom asked</u>.

'Actually,' <u>said Ali</u>, 'it's too cold to go to the beach.'

Usage activities

Spelling and vocabulary

A prefix can be added to a word to alter its meaning. Some prefixes will alter the word's meaning to its opposite, for example:

like – dislike

active – inactive.

HELP

A prefix is a group of letters or a letter added to the front of a word or root. For example, the prefix 're' means 'again', so if it is added to the base word 'build', 'to rebuild' would mean 'to build again'.

Activity

- Use these fifteen words to make a list of prefixes that change a word to its opposite meaning.

untrue	irregular	immobile
mislead	unfortunate	illegal
disobey	illegible	irresponsible
invisible	disbelieve	anticlockwise
impatient	uncertain	antiperspirant

- Can you come up with any rules about when to use each one?

Usage activities

Usage – Unit Two

Modal verbs

Modal verbs work with other verbs, for example:
- Could stay
- Should go
- Might ask
- May succeed

They are known as modal verbs because they signal some uncertainty about the action. It might happen, it might not.

Activity

- Complete the sentences below.
  We <u>may</u> go to the beach later if…
  We <u>might</u> let you go if…
  We <u>could</u> go if…
  We <u>would</u> go if…
  We <u>ought</u> to go if…
  We <u>should</u> go if…

Punctuation

You may have noticed in Unit Two that the longer narrative poems often use semicolons. They can be used instead of full stops to link short sentences. They make the reader look for the connection in meaning.

HELP

Examples

Sheba tugged hard at the great wooden door. The locks held tight.
(Two sentences.)

Sheba tugged hard at the great wooden door but the locks held tight.
(Using a conjunction.)

Sheba tugged hard at the great wooden door; the locks held tight.
(Using a semicolon.)

Usage activities

The following extract has commas and semicolons missing. Three of the brackets need a semicolon, the rest need commas. Read it carefully and decide which bracket needs a comma and which needs a semicolon.

> It was ten o'clock today that the first of all Time Machines began its career. I gave it a last tap [ ] tried all the screws again [ ] put one more drop of oil on the quartz rod [ ] and sat myself in the saddle. I suppose a suicide who holds a pistol to his skull feels much the same wonder at what will come next as I felt then. I took the starting lever in one hand and the stopping one in the other [ ] pressed the first [ ] and almost immediately the second. I seemed to reel [ ] I felt a nightmare sensation of falling [ ] and [ ] looking round [ ] I saw the laboratory exactly as before. Had anything happened? For a moment I suspected that my intellect had tricked me. Then I noted the clock. A moment before [ ] as it seemed [ ] it had stopped at a minute or so past ten [ ] now it was nearly half-past three!
>
> From *The Time Machine* by H. G. Wells

Spelling and vocabulary

A suffix is a letter, or group of letters put at the end of a word to change the way you use the word. A suffix can be added to a word to alter the way the word is used in a sentence.

I depend on my mum to get me up in the morning.
My mum is very dependable.

The suffix 'able' has changed 'depend' into an adjective.
There are other suffixes that mean a word is an adjective, such as:

-ic   -ible   -al.

Activity

- What are the base words to which suffixes have been added here?

comical	enthusiastic
perishable	horrible
comfortable	fantastic
tropical	profitable
sensible	miserable

Usage activities

Usage – Unit Three

Adverbial starts to sentences

An adverbial start to a sentence will tell the reader more about *where*, *when*, *why* or *how* the action happened. For example:

While she was on holiday, she decided to have her hair cut.
   adverbial beginning   *main clause*

This beginning tells you *where* the action took place.

Activity

- Put these adverbial beginnings into the correct list below. Four have been done for you.

By eleven o'clock,
Because she was bored,
Before breakfast,
At the door,
Surprisingly,
In response,
By the bus stop,
In order to look older,
At the last moment,
Grinning from ear to ear,
As a gesture of defiance,
During the discussion,
In the other room,
Without hesitation,
Over the way,
With great difficulty,
As a result of the conversation,
To spend the last of her money,
With some misgivings,
While she was on holiday,
When she was thirteen,
Back at the ranch,
Reluctantly,
Quickly,
In the supermarket,

Where	When	Why	How
At the door,	While she was on holiday,	In order to look older,	Quickly,

Usage activities

Punctuation

As shown in Unit Three, an editor sometimes needs to simplify a piece of writing. However, it is sometimes necessary to write using long sentences. Commas are useful when writing long sentences but it is important to know why and when they should be used.

> **HELP**
>
> Commas can be used for:
>
> 1. Lists – to separate items in a list of things, events and actions.
> 2. Drop-ins – to separate off an added clause or aside that is dropped into the main clause.
> 3. Extensions – to extend the main clause by adding another. Watch for the 'action' words.

Read the following text carefully. It is taken from a short story written over a hundred years ago when the fashion was to write using longer sentences.

Write out the text and use the numbers in the Help Box above to show if the comma is being used to show a list, a drop-in or an extension. The first one has been done for you.

I drew breath,[3] set my teeth,[ ] gripped the starter lever with both hands,[ ] and went off with a thud. The laboratory got hazy and went dark. Mrs. Watchets came in and walked,[ ] apparently without seeing me,[ ] towards the garden door. I suppose it took her a minute or so to traverse the place,[ ] but to me she seemed to shoot across the room like a rocket. I pressed the lever over to its extreme position. The night came like the turning of a lamp,[ ] and in another moment came tomorrow. The laboratory grew faint and hazy,[ ] then fainter and even fainter. Tomorrow night came black,[ ]then day again, [ ] night again,[ ] day again,[ ] faster and faster still. An eddying murmur filled my ears,[ ] and a strange dumb confusedness descended on my mind.

From *The Time Machine* by H.G. Wells

Usage activities

Spelling and vocabulary

The suffix 'ify' means that the word to which it is attached is a verb.
Can you find another suffix that automatically means the word is a verb?

> ### Activity
> - Check the meanings of these words and use each one in a sentence.
>
> | | |
> |---|---|
> | magnify | identify |
> | verify | classify |
> | clarify | justify |
> | amplify | beautify |
> | horrify | intensify |

Usage – Unit Four

Starting a new paragraph

Read this extract from *The Other Facts of Life* by Morris Gleitzman.

> Claire Guthrie keeled over and crashed to the kitchen floor. She lay motionless, eyes closed, arms splayed. [ ] Instead of sprinting to the phone, ringing an ambulance, sprinting back, giving Claire mouth to mouth, weeping, panicking and making silly deals with God, her mother merely sighed and plonked down a steak the size of Tasmania onto the kitchen table in front of Ben. [ ] 'Claire' said Di, longsufferingly. [ ] Ben wasn't too worried by his sister's collapse either. He thought she'd held the horrified stare at her plate a couple of seconds too long and one roll of the eyes before going down would have done but at the moment he was more interested in beef than ham. He stared thoughtfully at the two huge steaks steaming on the table. [ ] Claire's eyes snapped open and she dragged herself theatrically onto her chair. [ ] 'Sorry,' she said, 'it was just too much for me, the sight of three months' meals all on the one plate.'

Activity
- The brackets indicate where the paragraphs should begin.
- Use the Help Box to decide the reason for starting each paragraph.

HELP

Check out these reasons for starting a new paragraph:

1. When there is a change in subject
2. When there is a shift in time
3. When there is a change in viewpoint
4. When someone new starts to speak

Usage activities

Punctuation

Look back at the previous extracts from *The Time Machine* by H.G. Wells (pages 129 and 131). Now read the continuation of the story.

> I was already going too fast to be conscious of any moving things. The slowest snail that ever crawled dashed by too fast for me. The twinkling succession of darkness and light was excessively painful to the eye. Then [1] in the intermittent darknesses [2] I saw the moon spinning swiftly through her quarters from new to full [3] and had a faint glimpse of the circling stars. Presently [4] as I went on [5] still gaining velocity [6] the palpitation of night and day merged into one continuous greyness [7] the sky took on a wonderful deepness of blue [8] a splendid luminous colour like that of early twilight [9] the jerking sun became a streak of fire [10] a brilliant arch [11] in space [12] the moon a fainter fluctuating band [13] and I could see nothing of the stars [14] save now and then a brighter circle flickering in the blue.

Activity
- There are ten commas and four semicolons missing. Decide which bracket needs a comma and which needs a semicolon and try to explain your choices (see the Help Boxes on pages 128 and 131).

Spelling and vocabulary

The word 'paragraph' has a 'ph' sound, which is pronounced 'f'.

Activity
- Read the list of words below, they all contain the 'ph' sound. It can be at the beginning, in the middle or at the end of a word. These words are often borrowed from the Greek language.

pharmacy	photograph	physical	triumph
alphabet	orphan	atmosphere	prophet
epitaph	microphone		

- Can you add further words with the 'ph' sound?

Usage – Unit Five

Paragraph structure 1

One of the ways in which paragraphs are 'glued together' is through the use of pronouns. Pronouns can help make links between different ideas without repetition. Pronouns refer back to subjects that have already been introduced and those that will follow.

Compare the two paragraphs:

> The man went to take the man's dog for a walk. The man called Toto, the man's dog, and showed Toto Toto's lead. As the man and the dog were leaving the house, the man's daughter explained that the man's daughter would like to join the man and the dog for a walk.
>
> The man went to take his dog for a walk. He called Toto, his dog, and showed him his lead. As they were leaving the house, his daughter explained that she would like to join them for a walk.

Read the following paragraph:

> The teacher explained the rules of the game to the pupils. The pupils listened carefully as the pupils were excited about the opportunity to play a new game: water polo. The teacher asked the pupils to repeat the rules to the teacher. The pupils did; most of the pupils had understood the rules, but one of the pupils had not. Therefore, the whole class waited for the teacher's explanation and for the confused pupil to show the teacher that the pupil had now understood.

Write out the paragraph using pronouns to replace the highlighted words.

Usage activities

Punctuation

Colons and semicolons can be used to list clauses – or mini-sentences – in much the same way as commas can be used to divide items in a list.

Study the following extract.

> She took in many things all at once: that he spoke a broad Tirolean dialect; that some of his clothes might once have been part of a uniform but were now faded and worn; that he had tried to cut the shock of dark hair that hung down over his eyes; that he was at least a few years older than she was; and that a gun leaned against the wall within his immediate reach.
>
> From *Homestead* by Rosina Lippi

Notice that the colon [:] introduces a list. The semicolon [;] divides the items.

Write the following passage putting in the missing colon and semicolons.

> The mountain would shift lazily and open itself to reveal some small treasure the spire of rock that gave the Steeple its name a patch of gullies and ravines twisting like gnarled fingers the cowshed, weathered shingles glistening with wet.

Spelling and vocabulary

The suffix 'or' often turns the base word into a noun.

Activity

Read the word list.

governor	visitor	conductor	collector
sailor	radiator	survivor	actor
instructor	constructor		

- Can you add any more words with the suffix 'or'?
- Can you find another suffix that automatically means the word is a noun?

Usage activities

Usage – Unit Six

Paragraph structure 2

Connectives are used to 'glue' a paragraph together. They can be used to show links between ideas and how one idea leads into another.

Activity
- Work with a partner. Study the lists of connectives and try to decide what kind of job each group of words performs and when they might be used.
- Use the Help Box to give each group a heading. Two have been done for you.

Extend ideas			
Also	Firstly	Similarly	However
Moreover	Secondly	Likewise	On the other hand
Furthermore	Finally	By comparison	In comparison
Additionally	Later		An opposing view
	Next		Alternatively
	Then		
	After this		

Qualify ideas			
Although	For example	Consequently	In conclusion
Except for	Such as	As a result	As we have seen
Other than	For instance	So	To summarise
If only		Hence	In the end
		Therefore	Overall

HELP
Connectives can:
- Sequence actions
- Compare ideas
- Qualify ideas
- Link cause and effect
- Extend ideas
- Conclude
- Exemplify
- Contrast ideas

Usage activities

Rewrite the following paragraph using connectives to link the ideas.

> Puppies make wonderful pets. You can take a puppy for a walk. You can play games with it. Puppies are friendly. They are affectionate. They will cuddle up to you when you are feeling sad. You have to look after your puppy well. This requires time and money. He will need regular exercise. He will need the correct food and sufficient water each day. You will have to take him to the vet to receive his injections. You do not want him to get ill.

Punctuation

Write out the following passage as three paragraphs, adding the correct punctuation.

> four hundred and fifty years ago when queen elizabeth 1 was alive london was a very different place from the london of today london's muddy cobbled streets were very noisy people tried to sell their goods or advertise their trade by shouting things such as sweet lavender any frying pans to mend or buy buy you could buy custard coal apples sausages honey (not sugar) mouse traps and rabbits in fact you could buy almost anything on the streets of london.

Spelling and vocabulary

Knowing the meaning of a prefix can help you to work out the meaning of a word. The prefix 'sub' means 'under'.

Activity
- Check the meanings of these words.

submerge	subway
subdue	submarine
substandard	subordinate
subsoil	submissive
subnormal	subconscious

- What prefixes do you know that mean:

  over or above   across   between   around?

Usage activities

Usage – Unit Seven

Paragraph structure 3

Read the paragraphs below. Use the highlighted links to decide how the writer has structured them.

> **HELP**
>
> The topic of a paragraph may be structured by:
> - Order of importance
> - Order of event
> - Cause and effect

1. First, you separate the eggs and add the egg whites to the bowl. Then, you whip the egg whites until light and fluffy. After that, you gradually spoon in the caster sugar, beating the mixture further as the sugar is added.

2. A volcano is essentially a safety valve. Eruptions are the result of pressures building up in the molten rocks below the surface of the earth. These pressures seek escape through the weak spots in the earth's crust, causing cracks to open and lava to spill out. Violent eruptions are caused when the collection of hot gases at the mouth of the volcano are ignited. The mountain itself is created of molten lava which hardens in the cool air, and thus builds up a raised lip around the mouth of the eruption.

3. There is good sense in giving teenagers an allowance instead of pocket money. The first and most important reason is that it gives them first-hand experience of managing a budget and this is one of the key skills of adult life. It also allows them the flexibility to spend money on things that they – rather than their parents – want to buy. Even if things go wrong and the money is spent unwisely, then at least they learn to live with their mistakes and spend the money more responsibly in the future.

Usage activities

Activity

- Look again at the points made in the Usage Units Four to Seven about writing paragraphs. Use the bulleted points below to write coherent paragraphs in which the ideas are smoothly linked.

A.
- Elephants have ivory tusks
- Tusks are very valuable – for jewellery
- Poachers kill elephants to obtain their tusks

B.
- If your puppy is ill, you may need to take him to the vet
- The vet may prescribe medicine, such as antibiotics
- The best way to administer this is with a syringe
- Draw fluid into the syringe, then squirt down the puppy's throat

C.
- Tidying your room causes conflict in families
- Untidy bedroom: hated by parents
- Tidying one's room: hated by teenagers
- Many battles fought: how often, when, whose responsibility?
- Lucky: any family without this conflict

Usage activities

Punctuation

Write out the following extract as two paragraphs. Put in the missing capital letters, full stops and commas. Take care to give all the proper nouns capital letters.

> the hong kong university department of architecture recently built 835 solar panels on a school in park island in hong kong [ ] in may 2004 [ ] the kei wai primary school and its gleaming new photovoltaic (pv) arrays were officially opened by the permanent secretary for education [ ] fanny law [ ] the project was co-sponsored by the government's innovation and technology fund and the china light and power research institute [ ] the blue skies and brilliant sun enabled the school children to show off the potential of the photovoltaic technology to over 1,000 parents and guests present that day [ ] with assistance from sam lam and huey pang of the hong kong university's (hku) pv research team [ ] students described the benefits of the technology that generates power from sunlight using specially developed software which logs the electricity produced from the school's extensive roof arrays [ ]

Spelling and vocabulary

The letters 'ch' usually make the sound used in arch or the sound used in architecture.

Activity

- Divide the following words into the two different 'ch' sounds.

headache	school	chop	architect
choir	chill	chum	orchestra
stomach	inch		

- Find five more words that use 'ch' as it is used in 'arch'.
- Find five more words that use 'ch' as it is used in 'architecture'.
- Give the meaning of each of the following words as used in the passage:

  innovation   potential   assistance   generates

141

Usage activities

Usage – Unit Eight

Complex sentences

Compare the following two paragraphs.

> 1. It was her birthday. I had planned a surprise. I had booked a holiday. I was taking her to Amsterdam. We would travel by air. I picked her up from work. We drove to the airport. We were just in time. I showed my passport. She didn't have her passport. I was horrified. 'Have a nice time,' she said. I don't think she meant it.
> 2. I once planned a holiday for two in Amsterdam as a birthday surprise for her. I picked her up from work and drove to the airport, arriving just in time to show my passport and realise, to my horror, that I had forgotten to pack hers. 'Have a nice time,' she said, but I don't think she meant it.

What ways have been used to collapse the thirteen sentences in Paragraph 1 into three sentences in Paragraph 2?

HELP

Collapsing simple sentences into more complex ones may help to improve the style of the piece of writing. This can be done by:
- Joining sentences with a conjunction or semicolon
- Embedding a sentence within another sentence
- Merging sentences
- Finding a new way to convey the main information

Activity

- Collapse the following eleven sentences into two complex sentences.

> I travelled by bus. It was late. It was raining. She was standing outside the restaurant. She had been waiting for half an hour. She was furious. I tried to apologise. She wasn't listening. I tried again. She couldn't bring herself to speak to me. I was ashamed.

Usage activities

Punctuation

Read this extract from the Anthony Horowitz horror story *A Career in Computer Games* and then add the missing punctuation. Take care, the extract needs a lot of question marks!

---

please come in mr go said seeing kevin at the door he smiled revealing a row of teeth with more silver than white sit down he gestured at the chair and kevin took it feeling more suspicious by the minute there was definitely something odd here something not quite right mr go reached into his desk and took out a square of paper some sort of form kevin's reading wasn't up to much and anyway the paper was upside down but as far as he could tell the form wasn't written in english the words were made up of pictures rather than letters and seemed to go down rather than across the page it had to be japanese he supposed

what is your name mr go asked him

kevin graham

age

sixteen

address

kevin gave it

you've left school

yeah a couple of months ago

and tell me please did you get good gcses

no Kevin was angry now your ad said no qualifications needed that's what it said so why are you wasting my time asking me

mr go looked up sharply it was impossible to tell with the dark glasses covering his eyes but he seemed to be pleased

Usage activities

Spelling and vocabulary

Homophones are words that sound the same, but have different meanings.

Activity

- Match the meanings (below) to the words in the table. Take careful note of the spellings.

Word	Meaning	Word	Meaning
bear	an animal	allowed	
bare		aloud	
rain		course	
reign		coarse	
see		through	
sea		threw	
sites		braking	
sight		breaking	
affect		practice	
effect		practise	rehearse
source		too	
sauce		two	2
		to	

Meanings:

origin, result, places, salt water, naked, water droplets, observe, vision, influence, dressing for food, spoken to be heard, hurled, rough, dividing by force, rehearse, track, permitted, rehearsal, overly, stopping, 2, passed beyond, towards, an animal, to rule

Usage answers

Unit One – Conditionals

That's a lovely painting, Natalie. <u>When it's done,</u> we can put it on the wall. No, don't do that, or <u>I might take</u> the brush away. Put it down, Natalie. Natalie, put the brush down <u>or else I'll be cross</u>. Yes, I know George likes blue, <u>but not on his back</u>. Put it down! George's Mummy will be very cross <u>if she sees him</u> in that state. Now, don't cry, George. Thank you, Ali, that's very thoughtful of you. Let's get some water and see <u>if we can wash it off</u>. That's better. <u>If you behave,</u> we'll have a story.

Punctuation

The two friends sat down to drink from their cans and began to think of the end of term.

  'What are you going to do in the holidays<u>?</u>' <u>asked Clare</u>. 'Do you have any plans<u>?</u>'

  'I am going to stay with my cousins for a week<u>,</u>' <u>replied Julie</u>. 'I go every year. What about you<u>?</u>'

  'We hire a caravan and drive to the coast. We stay at the same place every year. It's great actually<u>,</u> but I get bored in the car.'

  <u>Julie agreed</u>. 'I think the best bit about holidays is being at home and having time to do things. I enjoy that as much as being away.'

  'I can't wait<u>,</u>' <u>said Clare</u>.

Unit Two – Punctuation

It was ten o'clock today that the first of all Time Machines began its career. I gave it a last tap[,] tried all the screws again[,] put one more drop of oil on the quartz rod[,] and sat myself in the saddle. I suppose a suicide who holds a pistol to his skull feels much the same wonder at what will come next as I felt then. I took the starting lever in one hand and the stopping one in the other[,] pressed the first[,] and almost immediately the second. I seemed to reel[;] I felt a nightmare sensation of falling[;] and[,] looking round[,] I saw the laboratory exactly as before. Had anything happened? For a moment I suspected that my intellect had tricked me. Then I noted the clock. A moment before[,] as it seemed[,] it had stopped at a minute or so past ten[;] now it was nearly half-past three!

Unit Three – Adverbial starts to sentences

Where	When	Why	How
At the door, In the supermarket, Back at the ranch, Over the way, In the other room, By the bus stop,	While she was on holiday, When she was thirteen, During the discussion, At the last moment, Before breakfast, By eleven o'clock,	In order to look older, To spend the last of her money, As a result of the conversation, As a gesture of defiance, In response, Because she was bored,	Quickly, Reluctantly, With some misgivings, With great difficulty, Without hesitation, Grinning from ear to ear, Surprisingly,

Usage answers

Punctuation

I drew breath,[3] set my teeth,[3] gripped the starter lever with both hands,[3] and went off with a thud. The laboratory got hazy and went dark. Mrs. Watchets came in and walked,[2] apparently without seeing me,[2] towards the garden door. I suppose it took her a minute or so to traverse the place,[3] but to me she seemed to shoot across the room like a rocket. I pressed the lever over to its extreme position. The night came like the turning of a lamp,[3] and in another moment came tomorrow. The laboratory grew faint and hazy,[3] then fainter and even fainter. Tomorrow night came black,[1]then day again,[1] night again,[1] day again,[1] faster and faster still. An eddying murmur filled my ears,[3] and a strange dumb confusedness descended on my mind.

Unit Four – Starting a new paragraph

Claire Guthrie keeled over and crashed to the kitchen floor. She lay motionless, eyes closed, arms splayed. [3] Instead of sprinting to the phone, ringing an ambulance, sprinting back, giving Claire mouth to mouth, weeping, panicking and making silly deals with God, her mother merely sighed and plonked down a steak the size of Tasmania onto the kitchen table in front of Ben. [4] 'Claire' said Di, longsufferingly. [3] Ben wasn't too worried by his sister's collapse either. He thought she'd held the horrified stare at her plate a couple of seconds too long and one roll of the eyes before going down would have done but at the moment he was more interested in beef than ham. He stared thoughtfully at the two huge steaks steaming on the table. [1] Claire's eyes snapped open and she dragged herself theatrically onto her chair. [4] 'Sorry,' she said, 'it was just too much for me, the sight of three months' meals all on the one plate.'

Punctuation

1 [,] it separates off an added clause
2 [,] it separates off an added clause
3 [,] it extends the main clause by adding another
4 [,] it extends the main clause by adding another
5 [,] it separates off an added clause
6 [,] it separates off an added clause
7 [;] it links a clause without using a conjunction
8 [,] it extends the main clause by adding another
9 [;] it is used instead of a full stop
10 [,] it separates off an added clause
11 [,] it separates off an added clause
12 [;] it links a clause without using a conjunction
13 [;] it is used instead of a full stop
14 [,] it separates off an added clause

Unit Five – Paragraph structure 1

The teacher explained the rules of the game to the pupils. They listened carefully as they were excited about the opportunity to play a new game: water polo. She/he asked them to repeat the rules to her/him. They did; most of them had understood them, but one of them had not. Therefore, the whole class waited for the teacher's explanation and for the confused pupil to show her/him that she/he had now understood.

Punctuation

The mountain would shift lazily and open itself to reveal some small treasure: the spire of rock that gave the Steeple its name; a patch of gullies and ravines twisting like gnarled fingers; the cowshed, weathered shingles glistening with wet.

Usage answers

Unit Six – Paragraph structure 2

Extend ideas	Sequence actions	Compare ideas	Contrast ideas
Also Moreover Furthermore Additionally	Firstly Secondly Finally Later Next Then After this	Similarly Likewise By comparison	However On the other hand In comparison An opposing view Alternatively

Qualify ideas	Exemplify	Link cause and effect	Conclude
Although Except for Other than If only	For example Such as For instance	Consequently As a result So Hence Therefore	In conclusion As we have seen To summarise In the end Overall

Punctuation

See page 83.

Unit Seven – Paragraph structure 3

1. order of event
2. cause and effect
3. order of importance

Punctuation

The Hong Kong University Department of Architecture recently built 835 solar panels on a school in Park Island in Hong Kong [.] In May 2004 [,] the Kei Wai Primary School and its gleaming new photovoltaic (PV) arrays were officially opened by the Permanent Secretary for Education [,] Fanny Law [.] The project was co-sponsored by the Government's Innovation and Technology Fund and the China Light and Power Research Institute [.]

   The blue skies and brilliant sun enabled the school children to show off the potential of the photovoltaic technology to over 1,000 parents and guests present that day [.] With assistance from Sam Lam and Huey Pang of the Hong Kong University's (HKU) PV Research team [,] students described the benefits of the technology that generates power from sunlight using specially developed software which logs electricity produced from the school's extensive roof arrays [.]

Unit Eight – Punctuation

'Please come in,' Mr Go said, seeing Kevin at the door. He smiled, revealing a row of teeth with more silver than white. 'Sit down!' He gestured at the chair and Kevin took it, feeling more suspicious by the minute. There was definitely something odd here. Something not quite right. Mr Go reached into his desk and took out a square of paper: some sort of form. Kevin's reading wasn't up to much and anyway the paper was upside down but as far as he could tell the form wasn't written in English. The words were made up of pictures rather than letters and seemed to go down rather than across the page. It had to be Japanese, he supposed. 'What is your name?' Mr Go asked him.
'Kevin Graham.'
'Age?'

147

Usage answers

'Sixteen.'
'Address?'
Kevin gave it.
'You've left school?'
'Yeah, a couple of months ago.'
'And tell me please. Did you get good GCSEs?'
'No.' Kevin was angry now. 'Your ad said no qualifications needed. That's what it said. So why are you wasting my time asking me?'
Mr Go looked up sharply. It was impossible to tell with the dark glasses covering his eyes, but he seemed to be pleased.

Spelling and vocabulary

Word	Meaning	Word	Meaning
bear	an animal	allowed	permitted
bare	naked	aloud	spoken to be heard
rain	water droplets	course	track
reign	to rule	coarse	rough
see	observe	through	passed beyond
sea	salt water	threw	hurled
sites	places	braking	stopping
sight	vision	breaking	dividing by force
affect	influence	practice	rehearsal
effect	result	practise	rehearse
source	origin	too	overly
sauce	dressing for food	two	2
		to	towards